TEAC[…]F

C000145612

Quick

ARABIC

Diethard Lübke and
A.H. Al-Sharqawi

Langenscheidt

Hodder & Stoughton
LONDON SYDNEY

A CIP catalogue record for this title is available from the British Library.

ISBN 0 340 55061 9

First published 1991 by Langenscheidt Publishers

Edited and typeset by The Arabic Advertising & Publishing Co. Ltd., London W1X 5LE.
Koranic quotations from 'The Koran', Penguin Classics, revised edition 1990.
Printed in Great Britain for the educational publishing division of Hodder and Stoughton Ltd, Mill Road, Dunton Green, Sevenoaks, Kent by Clays Ltd, St. Ives plc, Bungay, Suffolk.

Contents

Introduction

This course of self study aims to help you understand and speak simple Arabic, the sort which you will need on a visit to any Arab country. It cannot promise that at the end you will be speaking perfectly, but by enabling you to learn the most important words and expressions a visitor needs, it will undoubtedly help to improve your experience of the Arab country and get more out of your time abroad.

The course does not require a great deal of study, but it does offer more than a phrasebook and you will find that if you are prepared to spend a certain amount of time, even at odd hours of the day, in going through each unit in turn and testing your knowledge carefully, you will begin to acquire a basic knowledge of the language.

About six weeks before your trip, start looking at the Arabic script on pages 7–10. When you feel you have mastered this sufficiently, move on to the 20 units.

Each unit deals with a particular aspect of a visit to an Arab country, and contains groups of words and phrases in approximate transliteration in English phonetics, followed by English translations. Look at them carefully and read them aloud. If you have the cassette, look at the book as you listen, and practise repeating each word or phrase. The exercises that follow are to reinforce what you have learned and to test that you have grasped the basic language needed to cope with the situations most likely to occur. For example, as well as ordering food, making purchases, dealing with public transport and so on in simple Arabic, you are asked to work out the information given on a ticket and a shop notice, and to decipher simple street and road signs.

At the end of most units is a short information section in English which you will find useful on your visit. Take the book with you when you go to any Arab country so that you can practise the words and phrases you have learnt. Don't be afraid to use them – you are bound to make mistakes, but the most important thing is that you will have made yourself understood.

Arabic is spoken by about 150 million people in more than 20 countries. The regional dialects (which are in fact 'mother tongues') are very different from one another. So much so that many educated Arabs will say to you: 'Here we say it like this, but in correct Arabic you say it like this'.

In this course we concentrate on the so-called 'correct' Arabic which is understood everywhere – where this is not the case, the words which are in common usage in Morocco, Tunisia and Egypt are given.

A piece of advice: In 'Maghreb' i.e. in Morocco, Tunisia and Algeria, French is the second language. In Egypt and the other Arab countries, you will find that some people speak a small amount of English.

The Arabic Script

- Arabic is written from right to left.
- The appearance of the (approximately 28) characters depends on whether they occur at the beginning, in the middle or at the end of the word, also on whether they stand alone.
- Most characters are written in one stroke and only a few are not joined together. They are shown with an *.

	standing alone	at the end	in the middle	at the beginning	Notes
ā	ا	ـا	ـا	ا	long 'a', as in trap, bad
-a	ة	ـة			at the end of a word to show feminine form, as in comma
ʕ	ع	ـع	ـعـ	عـ	glottal voiced consonant like 'ah!' but deeper
b	ب	ـب	ـبـ	بـ	as in English
d	د	ـد	ـد	د	as in English
d	ض	ـض	ـضـ	ضـ	pronounced as heavy 'd'

The Arabic Script

	standing alone	at the end	in the middle	at the beginning	Notes
dh	ذ	ـذ	ـذ	ذ	‘th’ as in ‘this’ or ‘dh’ as in ‘Riyadh’
ẓ	ظ	ـظ	ـظـ	ظـ	pronounced as heavy ‘z’ or ‘dh’
f	ف	ـف	ـفـ	فـ	as in English
gh	غ	ـغ	ـغـ	غـ	‘rr’, trilled as in French
h	ه	ـه	ـهـ	هـ	as in English
h	ح	ـح	ـحـ	حـ	
ī		ـى	ـيـ		long ‘i’, only in the middle and at the end of words
j	ج	ـج	ـجـ	جـ	pronounced as hard ’g’ in Egypt or as ‘dg’ as in ‘fridge’
k	ك	ـك	ـكـ	كـ	as in English
kh	خ	ـخ	ـخـ	خـ	like ‘ch’ in the Scottish ‘loch’, but deeper
l	ل	ـل	ـلـ	لـ	as in English
m	م	ـم	ـمـ	مـ	as in English
n	ن	ـن	ـنـ	نـ	as in English
q	ق	ـق	ـقـ	قـ	hard ‘k’

	standing alone	at the end	in the middle	at the beginning	Notes
r	ر	ـر	ـر	ر	trilled ‘r’
s ṣ	س ص	ـس ـص	ـسـ ـصـ	سـ صـ	‘ss’ as in ‘toss’ heavy ‘s’
sh	ش	ـش	ـشـ	شـ	as in English
t ṭ	ت ط	ـت ـط	ـتـ ـطـ	تـ طـ	as in English heavy ‘t’
th	ث	ـث	ـثـ	ثـ	‘th’ as in ‘thumb’
ū		ـو	ـو		long ‘u’, only in the middle and at end of words
w	و	ـو	ـو	و	‘w’ as in ‘water’
y	ى	ـى	ـيـ	يـ	
z	ز	ـز	ـز	ز	‘s’ as in ‘rose’
ʾ				ء	short ‘a’ as in ‘apple’
Sign for doubling consonants:				◌ّ	

The Arabic Script

Look at how these Arabic words are written, and try to write them yourself.

Taxi = tāksī

.... تاكسي ← īskāt

Soap = ṣābūn

.... صابون ← nūbāṣ

Market = sūq

.... سوق ← qūs

Peace = salām

.... سلام ← māl(a)s

Mecca = Makka

.... مكّة ← akk(a)M

Sugar = sukkar

.... سكّر ← r(a)kk(u)s

NB The short vowels a, i, u (which have no script characters) change their pronunciation according to the consonants which surround them.
For example:

'flfl' = filfil *or*
fulful (*pepper*)

The accent (´) indicates where the stress falls in a word.

1.1 Yes, no. – 1.2 Greetings. – 1.3 Please, thank you. – 1.4 Mr, Mrs. – 1.5 The, I, you.

Ahlan wa-sahlan means *Welcome* اهلاً وسهلاً.
(Lit. You come as a friend and not as a foe, and you will have no trouble here)

1.1	náʕam	*yes*
	(in many dialects áywa)	
	lā	*no, not*

náʕam, min, fáḍlak	*yes please* (to a man)
náʕam, min fáḍlik	*yes please* (to a woman)
lā, shúkran	*no thank you*

1 General Expressions

1.2	sạbấh al-khayr	*good morning*
	máʕa 'ṣ-salấma	*goodbye*
	márḥaba	*welcome*

as-salāmu ʕaláykum	*hello* (*Lit.* Peace be with you)
wa-ʕaláykumu s-salấm	*hello* (*Lit.* Peace be with you too)

1.3	shúkran	*thank you*
	shukran jazī́lan	*thank you very much*
	min fáḍlak	*please* (to a man)
	min fáḍlik	*please* (to a woman)
	ʕáfwan	*excuse me/don't mention it*
1.4	sáyyid/sádá	*gentleman/gentlemen; Mr*
	sáyyida/sayyidất	*lady/ladies; Mrs*

yā sáyyidī	*Sir*

1.5	al-	*the*
	wa-	*and*
	ánā	*I*
	ánta	*you* (to a man)
	ánti	*you* (to a woman)
	-ī	*my*
	-nī	*me* (dative)
	-ak	*your, you* (to a man)
	-ik	*your, you* (to a woman)
	-kum	*your, you* (to men)

Áḥmad wa-Ḥásan	*Ahmed and Hassan*
man ánta?	*Who are you?*
ánā Peter	*I am Peter*
záwjatī Láylā	*My wife Laila*
ibnī Muḥámmad	*My son Mohammed*
ibnatī Fáṭima	*My daughter Fatima*

General Expressions 1

1. You are addressing a man: ....

2. You are greeting an Arab: ....

3. You are saying goodbye: ....

4. Muslims would greet each other with:

....

5. The answer to this greeting is:

....

You are talking to Ahmed. He introduced his children:

6. My son Mohammed:

....

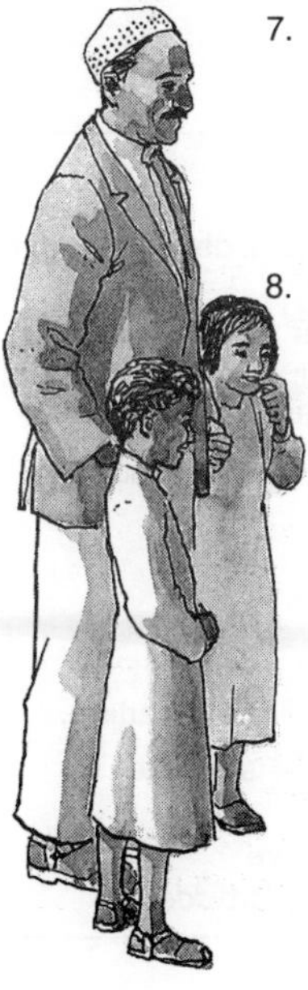

7. My daughter Fatima:

....

....

8. The tourist introduces his wife Sylvia:

....

....

General Expressions 1

Someone offers you an orange:

9. If you want it you say: ....

....

10. If you don't want it you say:

....

11. You want to excuse yourself: ....

....

- The article (*the*) is **al-** in Arabic
- When followed by one of the following: **d, dh, n, r, s, sh, t, th,** the **l** of the article changes:

a**l**-dār	› a**d**-dār
a**l**-Nīl	› a**n**-Nīl
a**l**-shāms	› a**sh**-shāms

- After words which end in a vowel, the **a** of the article is dropped:
  ayn**a**-'**l**-funduq?
  hatt**a** '**l**-masāʾ.
- The article is always written: ال
- *A, an* is expressed by a substantive without an article.
- The Arabic equivalent of the verb *to be* is not used in sentences like:

ánā hunā	*I (am) here.*
hādhā mamnūʕ	*That (is) forbidden!*

2.1 Customs. – 2.2 Documents. – 2.3 Nationality.

England = Ingiltrā
انجلترا ārtligni ←

Scotland = Iskutlandā
اسكتلندا ādnaltuksi ←

Wales = Waylz
ويلز zlyaw ←

Ireland = Irlandā
ارلندا ādnalri ←

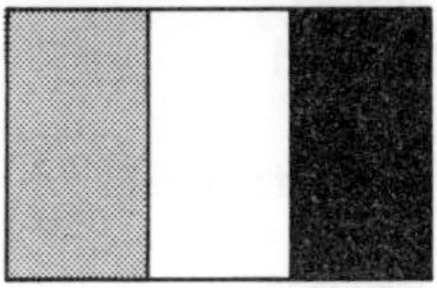

Morocco = al-Maghrib
المغرب b(i)(a)m-la ←

Tunisia = Tūnis
تونس s(i)nūt ←

Egypt = Miṣr
مصر rṣ(i)m ←

2 Entering An Arab Country

2.1	júmruk (Il Maghreb: jamárik)	*customs*
	murāqabat al-júmruk	*customs desk*
	haqība/haqā'ib	*suitcase*
	sak (Egypt, Syria: shánṭa)	*bag*

iftaḥ ash-shánṭa	*Open your bag*

2.2	jawáz } jawáz as-sáfar }	*passport*
	جواز السفر ← r(a)f(á)s-sa záw(a)j	
	ism	*name*
	ta'shíra, vísā	*visa*

al-jawáz, min fáḍlak	*Your passport please*
ism-ak? (m.) ism-ik? (f.)	*What's your name?*
ism-ī Aḥmad	*My name is Ahmed (Name-mine Ahmed)*

2.3	jinsiyya	*nationality*
	الجنسية ← ayy(i)sn(i)j-la	
	bilád	*country*
	Briṭánya al-ʕuzma	*Great Britain*
	Inglízī	*English*
	Iskutlándī	*Scottish*
	Wílzī	*Welsh*
	Irlándī	*Irish*
	jumhūriyya	*republic*
	mámlaka	*kingdom*
	sifára	*embassy*
	qunsuliyya	*consulate*

ánta inglízī	*Are you English?*
náʕam, ánā inglízī	*Yes, I'm English*
ʕáfwan,	*Excuse me,*
lā áfham sháy'an	*I don't understand* (*Lit.* not understand anything)
múmkin	*I'd like...*
atálfin li-l-qunsuliyya?	*... to phone the consulate*

Entering An Arab Country 2

You arrive in an Arab country.

1. A police official wants to see your passport. He says:

   ....

2. He asks you if you are English: ....

   ....

3. If you are, you answer: ....

   ....

4. It is obvious that he can't read your name properly so he asks you what your name is:

   ....

5. If your name is Smith, you reply:

   ....

مراقبة القمارق

CONTROLE DOUANE

6. What does this sign say? Read the Arabic text:

   ....

7. The (Egyptian) customs officer would like you to open your bag:

   ....

8. If you don't understand, you say:

   ....

What are these objects in Arabic?

9. .... 10. ....

What is this country called in Arabic?

11. ....

- There are almost no firm rules about forming the plural in Arabic. You need to learn the singular and plural for each noun.
- It is recommended that you take several copies of your passport before your journey and pack them in different places in your suitcase. Then, if you lose your passport, the procedures at the consulate will proceed a great deal more smoothly if you have a copy to hand.
- If you have a visa from Israel or South Africa in your passport, you will not be able to enter most Arab states.

3.1 Car. – 3.2 Petrol. – 3.3 Parking. – 3.4 Car hire.

Location de Voitures — كراء السيارات

	الوكالات Agencies	العنوان Adresse	الهاتف Téléph.
1	Europcar	Avenue du Koweit	80 146
2	Avis	Avenue du Koweit	80 303
3	Azur Rent a car	Rue Dag Hammarskjoeld	80 233
4	Hertz	Route des Hôtels	80 187

3 Travelling by car

3.1

sayyára/sayyārát	*car/cars*
karawán	*caravan*
motór	*motor*
fármala/farámil	*brake/brakes*
baṭṭāriya	*battery*
shámʕa/bujīh	*spark plug*
rādiyátōr	*radiator*
ʕájala/ʕajalāt	*wheel/wheels, tyre*

áyna garrāj ‘Peugeot’?	*Where is a Peugeot garage?*

3.2

maḥaṭṭat binzín	*petrol station*

محطّة بنزين ← nízn(i)b taṭṭ(a)ḥ(a)m

binzín	*petrol*
zayt motór	*motor oil*

áyna maḥáṭṭat al-binzín?	*Where is a garage?*
thalāthín litr, min fáḍlak	*30 litres, please*
ʕábbi, min fáḍlak	*Fill it up, please*

3.3

qif	*stop*
maḥáṭṭat sayyārát	*car park*
mamnúʕ al-wuqúf	*no parking*

3.4

kirāʾ as-sayyārát	*car hire*

áyna yúmkin . . .	*Where can I . . .*
. . . taʾjír sayyāra?	*. . . hire a car?*
uríd astáʾjir sayyára	*I would like to hire a car.*
kam as-siʕr . . .	*How much does it cost . . .*
. . . li-yawm wáḥid?	*. . . for one day?*
. . . li-thaláthat ayyám?	*. . . for 3 days?*
li-usbúʕ?	*. . . for a week?*
úktub hádhā, min fáḍlak	*Write that down, please.*

What is the Arabic for the following?

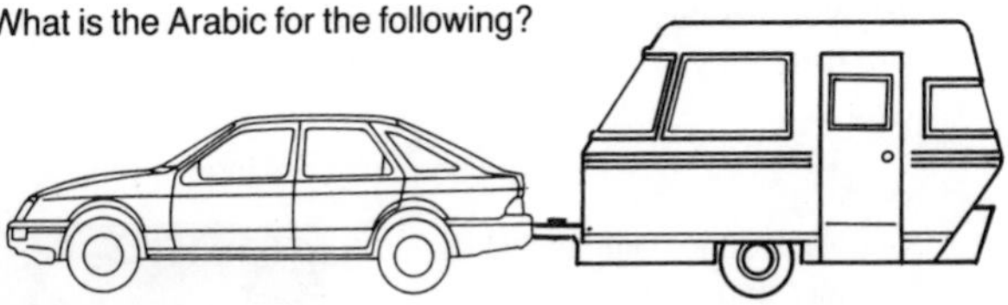

1. .... 2. ....

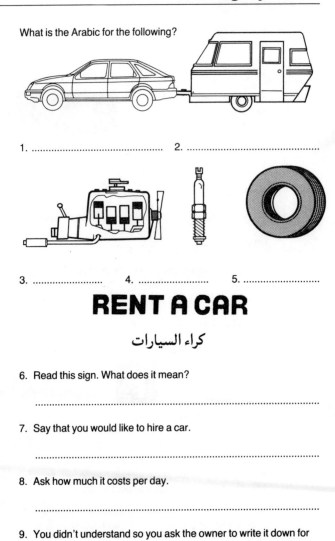

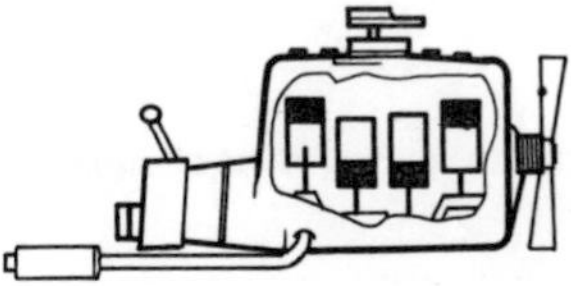

3. .... 4. .... 5. ....

RENT A CAR

كراء السيارات

6. Read this sign. What does it mean?

....

7. Say that you would like to hire a car.

....

8. Ask how much it costs per day.

....

9. You didn't understand so you ask the owner to write it down for you.

....

10. You are looking for a petrol station so you stop and ask a passer-by.

....

11. What's the name of this oil company?

....

12. You want 30 litres of petrol. What do you say to the pump attendant? ....

13. You want a full tank. What do you say to the attendant this time? ....

14. You have broken down, so you ask where a Peugeot garage is.

....

15. What does the policeman's sign mean? ....

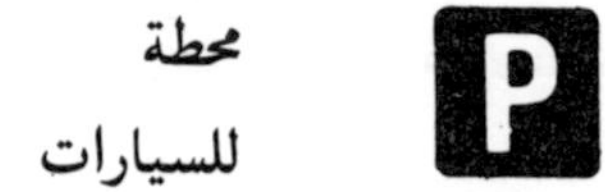

16. What does this traffic sign mean?

Give your answer in Arabic. ....

- Avoid driving at night. You risk having an accident with animals, children, vehicles without lights, etc.
- Remember that many North African drivers take a few risks. The number of people killed in road accidents is shockingly high.
- In Libya, traffic signs are written in Arabic only.

4.1 Map, town plan. – 4.2 Town/city, streets. – 4.3 Directions.

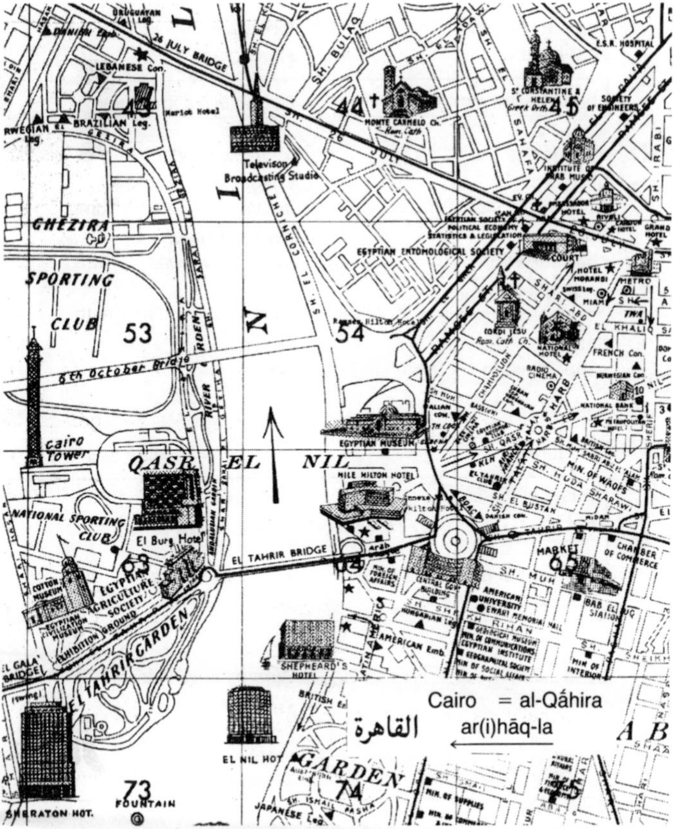

Cairo = al-Qâhira

القاهرة ← ar(i)hāq-la

Beirut = Bayrūt

بيروت ← tūry(a)b

Marrakesh = Marrâkesh

مرّاكش ← sh(e)kārr(a)m

Damascus = Dimashq

دمشق ← qsh(a)m(i)d

Tripoli = Tarābulus

طرابلس ← s(u)l(u)bār(a)t

4 Finding Your Way

4.1

kharița	*map*
خريطة ← ațir(a)hk	
kharitat al-madína	*town plan*
kharíțat țúruq	*street plan*
uríd kharíțat al-madína	*I would like a town plan*

4.2

madína	*(old) town, city*
qárya	*village*
bayt, dār	*house*
bāb	*gate, city gate*
sháriʕ/shawáriʕ	*avenue/avenues*
شارع ← ʕirásh	
nahj	*street*
sáḥa, maydán	*square*
ساحة ← aḥás	
țaríq/țúruq	*path/paths, country road*
wásaț al-madína	*city centre*
وسط المدينة ← anīd(a)m-la t(a)s(a)w	
ílā wásaț al-madína	*to the city centre*
țaríq saḥráwī	*desert track*

4.3

áyna ...?	*Where ...? Where is ...?*
(wēn, colloquial)	*Where are ...?*
húnā	*here*
hunák	*there*
(ʕálā) țúl	*straight on*
ʕal-yamín	*right*
ʕal-yasár	*left*
ílā	*to*
yálla!	*Go!*
áyna 't-țarík ílā Marrákesh?	*Where is the road to Marrakesh?*
áyna fúnduq 'Miramar'?	*Where is the hotel 'Miramar'?*

1. You want to buy a street map. You say to the assistant:

   ....

2. You ask a passer-by where the road to Tunis is:

   ....

3. You want to buy a town map. You say to the assistant:

   ....

4. You want to go to the city centre. You ask a passer-by:

   ....

In which direction do you go?

5. You are going into the city centre:

   ....

6. You are going to the Bab-Aleou square:

   ....

4 Finding Your Way

7. What is a construction like this called?

   ....

Read these originals. What do they say?

8. ....

9. ....

10. ....

In which directions are these arrows pointing?

اتجاه
اجباري
لليسار

اتجاه
اجباري
لليمين

11. .... 12. ....

5.1 Rail. – 5.2 Air. – 5.3 Ship. – 5.4 Urban Transport.

الخطوط الجوية التونسية

TUNIS AIR

Member of IATA International Air Transport Association

الخطوط الجوية الملكية الأردنية

THE ROYAL JORDANIAN AIRLINE

5 Public Transport

5.1

sikkat al-ḥadíd	*rail(way)*
maḥáṭṭa	*station*
tádhkara/tadhā́kir	*ticket/tickets*

تذكرة ← (a)r(a)kdh(á)t

uríd . . .	*I'd like*
. . . tádhkara ilā 'l-Qā́hira	*... a ticket to Cairo*
. . . tádhkaratáyn ilā al-Tū́nis	*... two tickets to Tunis*

5.2

maṭā́r	*airport*

مطار ← rāṭ(a)m

tayyā́ra	*aeroplane*
al-wuṣū́l	*arrival*
adh-dhahā́b/as-safar	*departure*
al-irshādāt	*information*

الارشادات ← tādāshri-la

tadhkarat tayyā́ra	*air ticket*
rā́kib	*passenger*
muḍífa	*stewardess*

5.3

safína	*ship*
kabína	*cabin*

5.4

bāṣ/bāṣā́t (Egyptian: otobís)	*bus/buses*
máwqif bāṣ (otobís)	*bus stop*
máwqif	*stop*
tā́ksī	*taxi*

تاكسي ← īskāt

máwqif tāksiyyā́t	*taxi rank*
jámal	*camel*

áyna máwqif al-bāṣā́t?	*Where can I find a bus stop?*
hā́dha 'l-bāṣ ilā Agadir?	*Is that the bus to Agadir?*
ilā 'l-maṭā́r	*to the airport*
ilā 'l-maḥáṭṭa	*to the station*
ilā fúnduq 'Ulysses'	*to the hotel 'Ulysses'*
kif húnā, min fáḍlak	*Stop here, please*
kam, min fáḍlak?	*How much, please?*

1. You have come off the plane and got into a taxi. Tell the driver that he should take you to the Hotel Meridian:

   ....

2. You are visiting someone so you tell the driver to stop here:

   ....

3. Ask him how much it costs:

   ....

4. Ask the driver to take you to the station:

   ....

5. You are in Alexandria and want a ticket to Cairo:

   ....

6. On another occasion you want two tickets to Cairo:

   ....

7. What do you call a ticket like this in Arabic?

   ....

5 Public Transport

8. You are looking for a taxi to take you to the airport.
   You ask a passer-by where the taxi rank is:

   ....

9. You tell the driver that you want to go to the airport:

   ....

10. At the airport you are looking for information. Which sign do you pay attention to?

    ....

11. You are looking for the departure point. Which sign do you follow?

    ....

12. Which animal is pictured on this stamp?

    ....

6.1 Hotel. – 6.2 Hotel room. – 6.3 Price. – 6.4 Toilet.

فندق تافوكت

HOTEL TAFOUKT

6 Accommodation

6.1 fúnduq, ōtēl (Maghreb: nuzl) — *hotel, hostel*

نزل ← lz(u)n فندق ← q(u)dn(u)f

istiqbál — *reception*

áyna 'i-fúnduq 'Miramar'	*Where is the hotel 'Miramar?'*
fúnduq al-maṭấr	*the airport hotel*

6.2

ghúrfa	*room*
saŕír/asírra	*bed/beds*
dūsh	*shower*
ḥammấm	*bath*
miftấḥ	*key*
miṣˤad	*lift*
ṭấbiq	*floor*

uŕíd . . .	*I'd like . . .*
. . . ghurfa li-shakhṣ wấḥid	*. . . a single room*
. . . ghurfa li-shakhṣáyn	*. . . a double room*
al-miftấḥ, min fáḍlak	*My key please*
raqm thalāthīn	*Number 30*

6.3 ath-tháman, as-siˤr — *the price*

الثمن ← n(a)m(a)th-tha

al fātúra, al-ḥisāb — *the bill*

حساب ← bās(i)ḥ فاتورة ← arūtāf

kam siˤr al-ghurfa li-yawm?	*How much does the room cost?*
al-ḥisấb, min faḍlak	*The bill please*

6.4 mirḥấḍ/marāḥíḍ — *toilet/toilets*

مرحاض ← ḍaḥr(i)m

waraq l-mirḥấḍ? — *toilet paper*

áyna l-mirḥấḍ?	*Where is the toilet?*
marāḥíd li-'r-rijál	*gentlemen's toilet*
marāḥíḍ li-s-sayyidất	*ladies' toilet*

1. You are looking for the hotel 'Miramar'. You ask a passerby:

....

2. Read the Arabic text on this sign. What does it mean?

....

3. Say that you would like a single room:

....

4. Say that you would like a double room:

....

5. You want to know the price per day. You ask:

....

What are these called in Arabic?

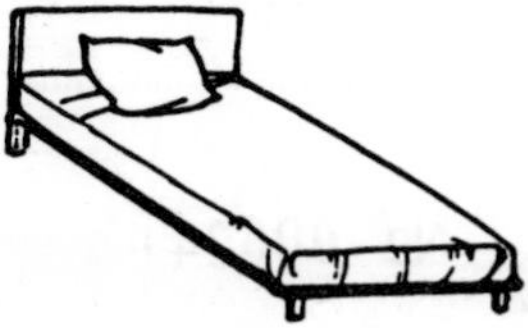

6. .... 7. ....

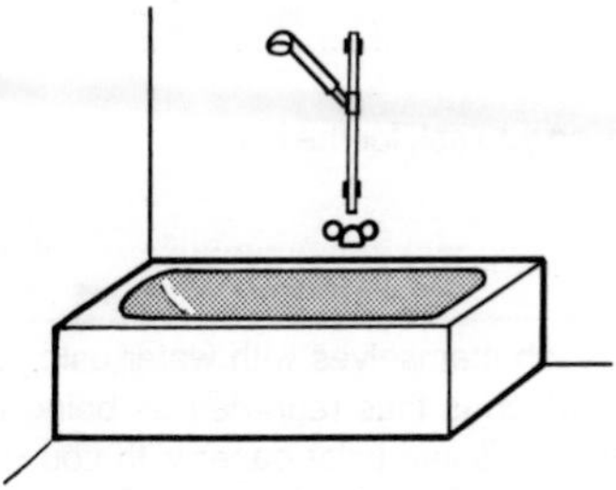

8. What do you call this room in Arabic?

....

9. Read the Arabic text on this sign:

....

10. Ask where the toilet is:

....

11. What's this in Arabic?

....

12. You return to your hotel and want your key. You say to the receptionist:

....

13. You are in room 30: ....

14. Read the Arabic word above. What does it mean?

....

15. You are about to leave, so you ask for the bill:

....

> In the toilet many Arabs wash themselves with water using the fingers of their left hand, which is thus regarded as being unclean. It is a good idea to take some toilet paper with you.

7.1 Counting. – 7.2 Weights and Measures.

1 = ١	11 = ١١	21 = ٢١	10 = ١٠	100 = ١٠٠
2 = ٢	12 = ١٢	22 = ٢٢	20 = ٢٠	200 = ٢٠٠
3 = ٣	13 = ١٣	23 = ٢٣	30 = ٣٠	300 = ٣٠٠
4 = ٤	14 = ١٤	24 = ٢٤	40 = ٤٠	400 = ٤٠٠
5 = ٥	15 = ١٥	25 = ٢٥	50 = ٥٠	500 = ٥٠٠
6 = ٦	16 = ١٦	26 = ٢٦	60 = ٦٠	600 = ٦٠٠
7 = ٧	17 = ١٧	27 = ٢٧	70 = ٧٠	700 = ٧٠٠
8 = ٨	18 = ١٨	28 = ٢٨	80 = ٨٠	800 = ٨٠٠
9 = ٩	19 = ١٩	29 = ٢٩	90 = ٩٠	900 = ٩٠٠

1000 = ١٠٠٠   1000 000 = ١٠٠٠ ٠٠٠

7.1

1	wā́ḥid	20	ʕishrī́n
2	ithnáin	21	wā́ḥid wa-ʕishrī́n
3	thalā́tha	22	ithnáin wa-ʕishrī́n
4	arbaʕa	30	thalāthī́n
5	khámsa	40	arbaʕī́n
6	sítta	50	khamsin
7	sābʕa	60	sittī́n
8	thamā́niya	70	sabʕī́n
9	tisʕa	80	thamānī́n
10	ʕáshara	90	tisʕī́n
11	iḥdā́ʕsh	100	miʾa
12	ithnā́ʕsh	200	miʾatáyn
13	thalāthá ʕsh	300	thalā́th miʾa
14	arbaʕtáʕsh	500	khams miʾa
15	khamstáʕsh	1000	alf
16	sittáʕsh	2000	alfáin
17	sabʕatáʕsh	3000	thalā́that ālā́f
18	thamāntáʕsh	1000000	milyū́n
19	tisʕatáʕsh		

miʾat dīnā́r (د)	*100 dinar*
khámsat darā́him	*5 dirham*
alf láyla wa-láyla	*1001 nights*
alf shúkr!	*A thousand thank yous!*

7.2

kam . . .	*How much/many . . .?*
litr	*litre*
ghrām (غ)	*gram*
kīlō	*kilo*
niṣf kīlō	*half a kilo*
mitr	*metre*
kīlumitr	*kilometre*

kīlō ṭamā́ṭim, min fáḍlak	*A kilo of tomatoes please*
kīlō burtuqā́l	*A kilo of oranges*
thalāthī́n litr	*30 litres*

In which hotel rooms are these hotel guests staying?

1. Ahmed: .... 2. Mohammed: ....

3. Mr Miller: .... 4. Miss Brown: ....

Read the numbers on these banknotes:

5. .... 6. .... 7. ....

8. What value is the banknote below?

....

9. From which country does it come?

....

10. Read the distances in Arabic:

You want to buy some things at the market:

11. You want to buy a kilo of tomatoes. What do you say to the stallholder?

....

12. You want to buy a kilo of oranges. What do you say to the stallholder?

....

8.1 Time. – 8.2 Times of the Day and Week.

Prayer times change daily. The first prayer hour is two hours before sunrise. **Allāhu** – The **-u** is the classical Arabic nominative ending.

8 Times and Dates

8.1

sā́ʕa	*hour*
daqī́qa/daqāʾiq	*minute/minutes*
khams daqāʾiq	*5 minutes*

kam as-sā́ʕa, min fáḍlak?	*What is the time please?*
كم الساعة ← aʕás-sa m(a)k	
ath-thā́niya	*It is 2 o'clock/At 2 o'clock*
as-sā́disa masā́ʾan	*At 6 p.m.*
ath-thā́niya wa-'n-niṣf	*At 2.30* (*Lit.* The 2 and a half)
aẓ-ẓuhr	*midday*

8.2

mátā . . .?	*When . . .?*
yawm/ayyā́m	*day/days*
ṣabā́ḥ	*morning*
ṣabā́ḥan	*in the morning*
masā́ʾ	*evening*
masā́ʾan	*in the evening*
láyla	*night*
layl	*night-time*
al-yawm	*today*
ams	*yesterday*
ghádan, bukra	*tomorrow*
al-ithnáyn	*Monday*
ath-thulāthā́ʾ	*Tuesday*
al-arbaʕā́ʾ	*Wednesday*
al-khamī́s	*Thursday*
al-júmʕa	*Friday*
as-sabt	*Saturday*
al-áḥad	*Sunday*

hátta 'l-masā́ʾ	*until this evening*
ghádan ṣabā́ḥan	*tomorrow morning*

What's the Arabic for . . .

1. . . . the time of day from sunrise to sunset?

....

2. . . . the half of the day between sunset and sunrise?

....

3. . . . a 60 minute period?

....

4. . . . a 60 second period?

....

5. You want to know what time it is. How do you ask?

....

What is the time?

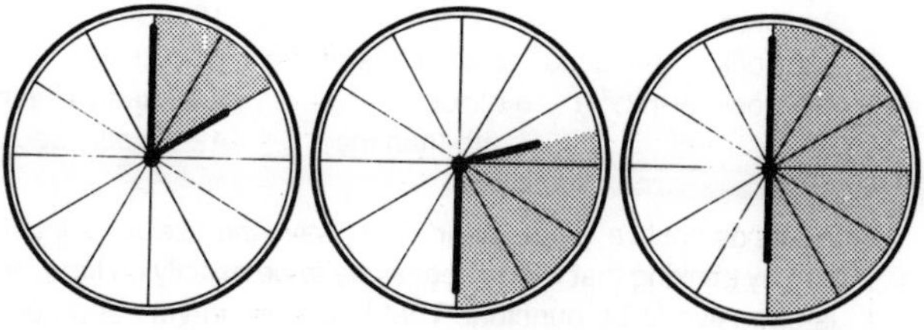

6. .... 7. .... 8. ....

9. How do you say 12 o'clock in Arabic?

....

8 Times and Dates

10. Read these days of the week in Arabic.

20 الأحد
Dimanche
21 الاثنين
Lundi
22 الثلاثاء
Mardi
23 الاربعاء
Mercredi
24 الخميس
Jeudi
25 الجمعة
Vendredi
26 السبت
Samedi

11. You are making a date for this evening:

....

12. You are making a date for tomorrow morning:

....

– The time is expressed with the feminine form of the number, except with 1:

1 o'clock: al-wấḥida	5 o'clock: al-khấmisa	9 o'clock: at-tấsiʕa
2 o'clock: ath-thấniya	6 o'clock: as-sấdisa	10 o'clock: al-ʕấshira
3 o'clock: ath-thấlitha	7 o'clock: as-sấbiʕa	11 o'clock: al-ḥấdiya ʕashar
4 o'clock: ar-rấbiʕa	8 o'clock: ath-thấmina	12 o'clock: aẓ-ẓuhr

– Arabs do not live 'by the hour'. They save themselves a lot of frustration by thinking that it isn't necessary to be exactly on time, and that it is obtrusive to be punctual. That is true for private and public life.
– The Islamic calendar began on June 16 622, the day that Mohammed left Mecca for Medina.
– The Islamic 'moon year' has 354-355 days. That is 10-12 days shorter than a 'sun year'. The twelve months go from new moon to new moon.
– The weekly day of rest is Friday (in Algeria, Libya and Saudi Arabia) or Sunday (Morocco and Tunisia).

9.1 Money. – 9.2 Changing money. – 9.3 Buying things. – 9.4 Paying.

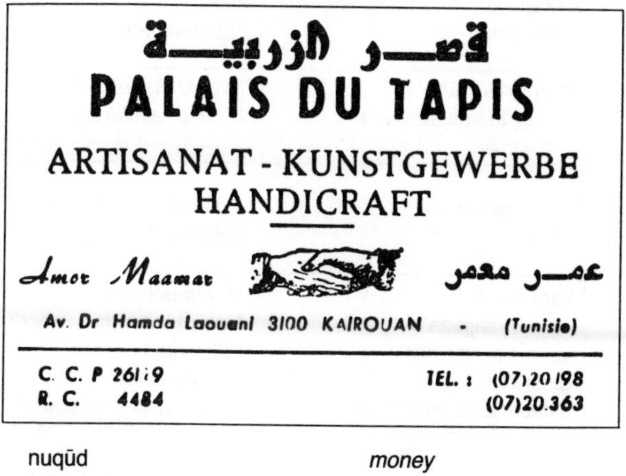

قصر الزربية
PALAIS DU TAPIS
ARTISANAT - KUNSTGEWERBE
HANDICRAFT
Amor Maamar
عمر معمر
Av. Dr Hamda Laouani 3100 KAIROUAN - (Tunisie)
C. C. P 261:9
R. C. 4484
TEL. : (07)20 198
(07)20.363

9.1	nuqūd	*money*
	fulūs (colloquial)	*money*
	dīnā́r/danānī́r	*dinar/dinars* (Algeria, Tunisia)

9 Money and Shopping

dirham/daráhim	*dirham/dirhams*
ginē/ginēhát	*pound/pounds*
ghaní	*rich*
faqír	*poor*

ánta ghanī	*You are rich*
ánā faqír	*I am poor*

9.2 bank — *bank*

بنك kn(a)b ←

ṣarf — *bureau de change*

صرف fraṣ ←

áyna 'l-bank?	*Where is the bank?*
uríd ṣarf an-nuqúd	*I would like to change some money*
uríd sarf khams miʾat giné	*I would like to change £50*

9.3

sūq	*market, bazaar*
dukkán	*shop*
súpermarket	*supermarket*

múmkin ashúf . . .	*I would like to have a look. . .*
as-sajjáda/as-surbíyya al-jamíla	*at the beautiful carpet*

9.4

as-siʕr, ath-tháman	*the price*
ghálī	*expensive*

kam as-siʕr?	*How much is it?*
kam as-sajjáda?	*How much is the carpet?*
khams miʾat dīnár	*500 dinar*
ghálī kathīr!	*very expensive!*
úktub hádhā, min fáḍlak!	*Please write that down!*

Money and Shopping 9

1. You are looking for a bank, so you ask a passerby:

....

2. You want to change some money. Which sign do you look out for?

CHANGE

صرف

....

3. You want to change £500. What do you say?

....

What are the currencies in:

4. Morocco?

5. Algeria?

....

6. Tunisia?

7. Egypt?

....

سوق

8. You are walking around the market and you see a beautiful carpet. You want to have a closer look. What do you say?

....

....

9. You want to know how much it costs. What do you say?

....

10. Ask the stallholder to write the price down for you:

....

11. He replies 500 dinar: ....

12. You reply that the carpet is very expensive:

....

13. You say to him that he is rich and you are poor:

....

14. After a long bargain you tell him that you will take it:

....

- In the markets and small shops, bargaining is generally acceptable. When a price is quoted to you, pretend to be astonished. Offer 10–20% of the price quoted and finally agree on 50% of the price.
- Banks are open from 9–11 o'clock.
- In tourist areas be very careful with your money. Cunning pickpockets are everywhere. Divide your money up and carry it in several places. Don't have it on view but do have a small amount to hand for drinks, tips, etc.
- In most Arab countries it is illegal to take in or bring out local currency.

10.1 Meals. – 10.2 Tableware. – 10.3 Breakfast.

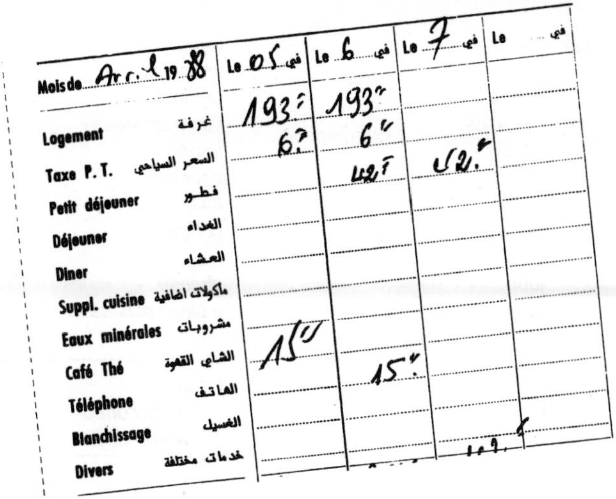

Mois de Avril 19 88	Le 05 في	Le 6 في	Le 7 في	Le في
Logement غرفة	193	193		
Taxe P. T. السعر السياحي	6	6		
Petit déjeuner فطور		42	52	
Déjeuner الغداء				
Diner العشاء				
Suppl. cuisine مأكولات اضافية				
Eaux minérales مشروبات				
Café Thé الشاي القهوة	15	15		
Téléphone الهاتف				
Blanchissage الغسيل				
Divers خدمات مختلفة			[illegible]	

10 Meals

10.1

akl	*food*
fuṭū́r	*breakfast*
ghadā́ʾ	*lunch*
ʕashā́ʾ	*dinner*

qā́ʕat al-akl	*dining room*
áyna qā́ʕat al-akl	*Where is the dining room?*

10.2

finjā́n	*cup*
kās	*glass*
zujā́ja	*bottle*
saḥn	*plate*
mílʕaḳa	*spoon*
sháwka	*fork*
sikkīn	*knife*
ibrī́q	*can/pot*

zujā́ja kabī́ra	*large bottle*
zujā́ja ṣaghī́ra	*small bottle*
ibrī́q ash-shāy	*teapot*

10.3

khubz	*bread*
kroasṓn	*croissant*
zúbda	*butter*
murábbā	*jam/marmalade*
ʕásal	*honey*
lában	*sour milk*
ḥalī́b	*milk*
qáhwa	*coffee*
shāy	*tea*
jubn	*cheese*
júbna	*a piece of cheese*

áʕṭinī . . .	*I'd like a . . .*
. . . qáhwa sā́da	*. . . black coffee*
. . . qahwa bi-' l-ḥalī́b	*. . . white coffee*

What are these meals called in Arabic?

1. Morning: ....

2. Lunchtime: ....

3. Evening: ....

What are these pieces of tableware?

4. ....

5. ....

6. ....

7. ....

8. ....

9. ....

10. ....

Read these Arabic words:

قهوة

حليب

11. .... 12. ....

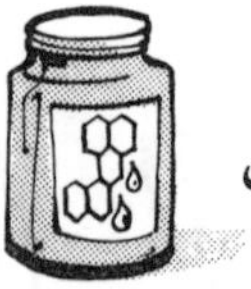

عسل

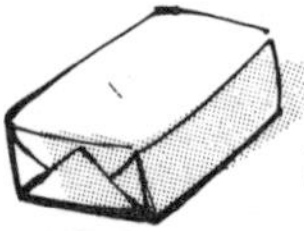

زبدة

13. .... 14. ....

- To avoid a stomach upset it is a good idea only to eat cooked and well-done meat, cooked vegetables and fruit which you can peel. Only drink hot drinks or water from unopened bottles.
- Many dishes (salad, dips) are served with a piece of round, flat bread which is used as a spoon.
- During Ramadan, Muslims must eat nothing between sunrise and sunset. Many restaurants close during this period. You should take this break into consideration when planning your trip.

Koran 2. (verse 185): In the month of Ramadan the Koran was revealed, a book of guidance with proofs of guidance distinguishing right from wrong. Therefore whoever of you is present in that month let him fast. But he who is ill or on a journey shall fast a similiar number of days later on. Allah desires your well being, not your discomfort. Eat and drink until you can tell a white thread from a black one in the light of the coming dawn. Then resume the fast till nightfall.

11.1 Restaurant, service. – 11.2 Seasonings. – 11.3 The bill.

مطعم عمر

RESTAURANT AMAR

مشهور في الاطعمة المغربية

GRANDES SPECIALITES DES PLATS MAROCAINS
FIRST CLASS COOK SPECIALISING IN MOROCCAN COOKING
ORIGINAL MAROKANISCHE SPEZIALITATEN
COMIDAS TIPICAS MARROQUIES

شارع تطوان رقم 30
30, Rue Tétouan

الحسيمة (المغرب)
AL HOCEIMA (Maroc)

Imp. Tuzani - Al - Hoceima

11 Restaurants

11.1	máṭʕam	*restaurant*
	مطعم ← m(a)ʕṭ(á)m	
	máqhā	*cafe*
	مقهى ← āhqam	
	ḥilwiyyā́t	*desserts/sweets*
	muraṭṭibā́t	*refreshments*

yāsáyyid	*Waiter!*
urī́d ā́kul shayʾ.	*I'd like something to eat.*
mā́dhā turī́d an tá'kul?	*What would you like to eat?*
mā́dhā turī́d an táshrab?	*What would you like to drink?*

11.2	súkkar	*sugar*
	سكّر ← r(a)kk(u)s	
	milḥ	*salt*
	ملح ← ḥlim	
	fílfil	*pepper*
	thūm	*garlic*
	zayt	*oil*
	khall	*vinegar*
	kammū́n	*cumin*
	kuzbara	*coriander*
	harī́sa	*hot paste made from paprika, spices and garlic* (for sauces and couscous)
	ḥārr	*hot*

11.3	ḥisáb, fātū́ra	*bill*
	فاتورة ← arūtāf	
	bakhshī́sh	*tip*

urī́d ádfaʕ.	*I'd like to pay*
al-ḥisā́b, min fáḍlak.	*The bill, please.*
kam hādhā?	*How much is it?*
hā́dhā lak.	*That's for you (that for you).*

1. Where do you go to eat lunch or an evening meal?

....

2. Call the waiter.

....

3. Tell him that you would like something to eat.

....

4. The waiter asks you what you would like to drink.

....

Read these Arabic words out loud:

5. .... 6. ....

7. When you have finished your meal, ask for the bill:

....

8. You leave the waiter a tip and say:

   ....

What are these spices called?

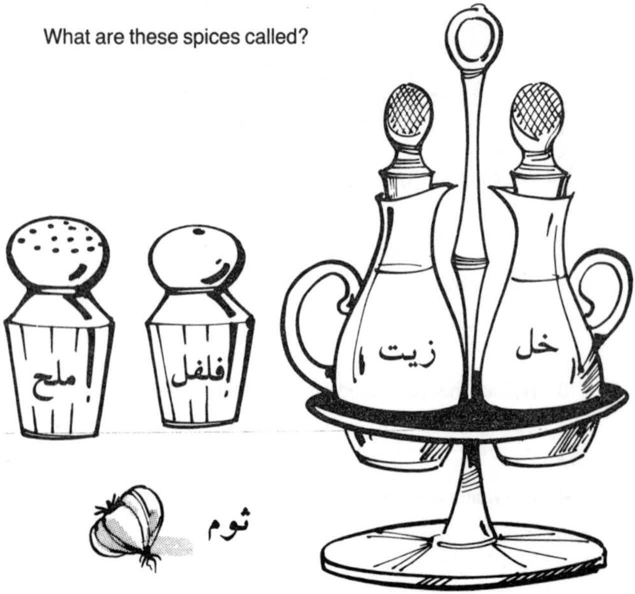

- In Arab countries, the cafe is a meeting place for men.
- The hot spices used in Arab cooking may speed up your digestion and may loosen your bowels. Perspiration causes a loss of minerals which are replaced by hot spices and salt.
- In most Arab countries, you should leave a tip at every opportunity. It is required to ensure good service. Do not give much to the hotel staff, but otherwise be generous. Tourists can afford to pay for a trip abroad and are therefore regarded as being 'rich'. Arabs regard it as a religious duty for a rich man to give to charity.

12.1 Soups. – 12.2 Meat. – 12.3 Poultry. – 12.4 Fish.

Lamb kebabs كباب (kabāb)
(for 4 people)

750 grams lamb fillet	Dice the meat and place it in a saucepan.
olive oil *2 table spoons lemon juice* *2 tea spoons coriander (crushed)* *2 tea spoons saffron* *1 tea spoon ginger* *2 tea spoons caraway* *salt* *pepper*	Blend everything to a marinade and pour over the meat. Leave in the fridge for 12 hours.
1 lemon	Allow the meat to drain and place on 4 skewers alternately with slices of lemon. Grill the skewers for 6–8 minutes and serve hot.

12 Soups, Meat, Fish

12.1 shúrba — *soup*

شوربة ← abrūsh

zaytún	*olives*
makarúna	*noodles/macaroni*

12.2 laḥm — *meat*

لحم ← mḥ(a)l

láḥma	*a piece of meat*
kharúf	*mutton*
laḥm kharúf	*lamb*
laḥm baqar	*beef*
stēk	*steak*
eskalóp	*schnitzel*
kabáb	*lamb kebab*
kabáb bi-'r-ruzz	*kebab with rice*
kíbda	*liver*

12.3 dajája/daját — *chicken/chickens*

دجاج ← jāj(a)d

báyḍa/bayḍ	*egg/eggs*
omlét	*omelette*

dajáj bi-'r-ruzz	*chicken with rice*
dajáj mashwī	*grilled chicken*

12.4 sámaka/sámak — *fish*

سمك ← k(a)m(a)s

sardína	*sardine*
tūn	*tuna fish*

تون ← nūt

áʕṭinī . . .	*I'd like some . . .*
. . . sámak máshwī	*. . . grilled fish*

The waiter is taking your order.

1. For example, you want to eat some noodles:

   ....

2. You want to eat a schnitzel:

   ....

3. You want to eat some liver:

   ....

4. You want to eat some grilled fish:

   ....

5. You want to eat some chicken with rice:

   ....

6. You want to eat an omelette:

   ....

12 Soups, Meat, Fish

What is being served below?

7. .... شوربة

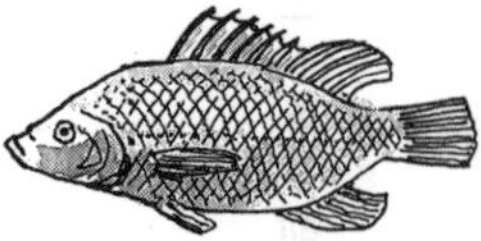

8. .... سمك

9. .... خروف

What kinds of food are pictured on this stamp?

10. ....

11. ....

- For a Muslim, pork is impure. Thus, pork is not eaten in any Arab country.
- The most popular meats in Arab countries are lamb and poultry. There is also beef.

Koran 16.
Eat of the good and lawful things which God has bestowed on you and give thanks for His favours if you truly serve Him.
He has forbidden you carrion, blood, and the flesh of swine; also any flesh consecrated other than in the name of God. . .

13.1 Vegetables. – 13.2 Fruit. – 13.3 Desserts.

Tajín
Tajin (*for 4 people*)

طجين

750 grams lamb	Chop into large pieces and place in a saucepan.
4 table spoons oil *1 tea spoon ginger* *1 tea spoon saffron* *salt* *pepper* *water*	Put the oil and spices into the pan. Fill with water until the meat is covered. Cook the meat until it is completely done. Remove it from the pan and allow to stand.
1 kg green peas *1 table spoon lemon juice* *6 pickled olives*	Cook quickly in the meat stock and then pour into a Tajin bowl (with a pointed lid). Place the meat and olives on top and serve hot.

Vegetables, Fruit, Desserts 13

13.1	khúḍar khuḍrawát	*vegetables*
	jázar	*carrots*
	baṭáṭā	*potatoes*
	ṭamáṭim	*tomatoes*
	báṣal	*onions*
	bisilla	*peas*
	lúbiyā	*beans*
	kuskus	*couscous*
	كسكس ← suk suk	
	ruzz	*rice*
	sálaṭa	*salad*

sálaṭat ṭamáṭim	*tomato salad*
ruzz bi-'l-ḥalíb	*rice pudding*

13.2	burtuqála/burtuqál	*orange/oranges*
	mawza/mawz	*banana/bananas*
	tamr	*dates*
	baṭṭíkha/baṭṭíkh	*melon/melons*
	tuffáḥa/tuffáḥ	*apple/apples*
	míshmish	*apricots*
	laymúna/laymún	*lemon/lemons*
	lawz	*almonds*
	zabíb	*raisins*

13.3	shokōláta	*chocolate*
	gató, kaʕk	*biscuits*
	jiláti, búẓa	*ice cream*
	baqláwa	*puff pastries*

uríd . . .	*I'd like . . .*
. . . kās búẓa.	*. . . a portion of ice cream*
khámas burtuqál, min fáḍlak.	*Five oranges, please.*
kílō ṭamáṭim, min fáḍlak.	*1 kilo of tomatoes, please*

What are these in Arabic?

ليمون

1. ....

برتقال

2. ....

بصل

3. ....

بطاطا

4. ....

مشمش

5. ....

طماطم

6. ....

بطيخ

7. ....

موز

8. ....

13 Vegetables, Fruit, Desserts

9. Read the Arabic text.
   What does it mean?

   ....

You are at the weekly market and are buying fruit:

10. a melon: ....

11. 5 oranges: ....

12. 1 kilo of tomatoes: ....

– Couscous is the national dish of North Africa, especially in Morocco and Tunisia. The ingredients are semolina, vegetables, lamb/chicken, and a piquant sauce. The dish is cooked in a two-storey couscous saucepan: in the bottom part are the vegetables. The rising steam cooks the semolina in the top part. The cooked semolina is served in a circle in a bowl with the vegetables and meat in the centre. The semolina is eaten with the thumbs, forefingers and middle fingers of the right hand formed into a scoop and brought up to the mouth.

– Arabs love desserts: honey, dates, marzipan, sweet marmalade, sweet pastries of all sorts. The most famous is baqlawa. This cake consists of 3 layers: at the bottom, about 10 wafer-thin layers of puff pastry; the middle a 1.2 cm wide lump of almonds and sugar (half and half) with a little cinnamon, and moistened with rose water; on top, another 10 wafer-thin layers of puff pastry. Baqlawa is baked at a moderate heat, and after half the baking time a thick syrup made of rosewater and sugar is poured over it. The following day it can be cut into 3 × 3 trapeziform pieces. (In fact, baqlawa is a typical wedding cake.)

14.1 Alcohol-free drinks. – 14.2 Alcoholic drinks. – 14.3 Smoking

14 Drinking, Smoking

14.1

mashrū́b	*drink/drinks*
qáhwa	*coffee*
قهوة ← awhaq	
shāy	*tea*
ḥalīb	*milk*
māʾ	*water*
māʾ li-'sh-shurb	*drinking water (water for drinking)*
māʾ máʕdinī	*mineral water*
ماء معدني ← īnidaʕ(a)m ʾām	
ʕaṣī́r	*juice (pressed)*
ʕaṣī́r al-burtuqā́l	*orange juice*
sharā́b al-burtuqā́l	*orangeade*
gazṓza	*lemonade*

شاي

áʕṭinī	*I'd like*
. . . shāy bi-'laymū́n.	*. . . lemon tea.*
شاي بالليمون ← nū́my(a)l-ib yāsh	
. . . qáhwa ḥílwa.	*. . . coffee with sugar.*
wā́ḥid kōlā, min fáḍlak.	*A cola, please.*

14.2

nabī́dh, khamr	*wine*
bī́ra	*beer*
konyák	*cognac*

ʕíndak bīra?	*Do you serve beer?*
wā́ḥid bī́ra, min fádlak.	*A beer, please*

14.3

tadkhī́n	*smoking*
sigā́ra/sagā́yer	*cigarette/cigarettes*
سجائر ← reyāg(a)s	
tábagh, dukhā́n	*tobacco*
دخان ← nāhk(u)d	
shī́sha, nargī́la	*hookah*
kibrī́t	*matches*

mamnū́ʕ at-tadkhī́n	*No smoking.*

1.
What are these drinks which you know from home?

....

The waiter is taking your drinks order.

2. Mineral water

....

3. A cola

....

4. Lemonade

....

5. Orange juice

....

6. Lemon tea

....

7. Coffee with sugar

....

8. Ask the waiter if he serves beer.

....

The name of the beer sign is pronounced 'bira stella'.

9. Order this beer:

....

10. Read these Arabic words. What do they mean?

....

Boissons non Alcoolisées

Café (express-filtre)	0 450	قهوة اكسبراس
Café au Lait	0 600	قهوة حليب
Café Glacé	0 600	قهوة مثلّجة
Thé au Citron	0 400	شاي بالقارص
Thé au Lait	0 500	شاي بالحليب
Chocolat	0 400	شكلاطة
Chocolat au Lait	0 700	شكلاطة بالحليب
Infusion	0 500	طرنجية
Lait	0 500	حليب
Capucin	0 500	كابوسن
Capucino	0 650	كابوشينو

- Muslims drink no alcohol because the Koran forbids it. Also you should not offer it to an Arab friend, because it would cause offence.
- Whisky, cognac, gin, etc. are very expensive everywhere and tourists will only find them in hotel bars, discos or night clubs. Drunken tourists are frowned upon and even punished in several Arab countries.
- Drug trafficking is severely punished in all Arab countries.

Koran 5.
Believers, wine and games of chance, idols and divining arrows are abominations devised by Satan. Avoid them, so that you may prosper. Satan seeks to stir up enmity and hatred among you by means of wine and gambling, and to keep you from the remembrance of God and from your prayers.

15.1 Tourism. – 15.2 Attractions. – 15.3 Events. – 15.4 Entrance.

15 Sightseeing

15.1	sáfar	*journey*
	riḥlāt	*excursions, trips*
	رحلات ← tālḥ(i)r	
	dálíl as-suwwáḥ	*guide book*
15.2	āthār	*antiquities*
	mát-ḥaf	*museum*
	al-mát-ḥaf al-misrī	*the Egyptian Museum*
	المتحف المصري ← irṣ(i)m-la f(a)ḥt(a)m-la	
	qaṣr	*palace*
	háram/ahrám	*pyramid/pyramids*
	ábu 'lhawl	*Sphinx*
	jámiʕ	*large mosque*
	bīr	*fountain*
	mádrasa	*school*
	máʕbad	*temple*
	qáṣba	*old quarter*
	bāb al-madína	*city gate*
	kabír	*large*
15.3	diskoték	*disco*
	sínamā	*cinema*
	nádī láylī	*night club*
	raqṣ shárqī	*belly dance* (oriental dance)
	al-ʕīd al-kabír	*sacrificial feast* (large feast 2 months after Ramadan)
15.4	maftúḥ	*open*
	مفتوح ← ḥūtf(a)m	
	khurúj	*exit*
	خروج ← jūr(u)kh	
	dukhúl	*entrance*

tadhkarat ad-dukhúl	*entrance ticket*
ayna bāb al-khurúj?	*Where is the exit?*

1. What's the Arabic name for this city?

....

2. Which country is it in now?

....

3. In which country is this temple?

....

15 Sightseeing

4. What is the Arabic name for this famous dance?

   ....

Read these signs. What do they mean?

رحلات

5. ....

مفتوح

6. ....

خروج

7. ....

8. What is this ticket for?

   ....

Islamic art. The Koran forbids painting of God, people and animals. This rule has left a very deep mark on Islamic art, of which a typical example is the Moorish style with its horseshoes, geometric figures, ornaments, arabesques, and so on.

16.1 Islam. – 16.2 Worship. – 16.3 Customs.

The Saudi flag contains the Islamic creed and the sword as a symbol of the defence of faith. The creed reads:
Lā ilāha illā Allāh, Muḥammad rasūlu Allāh . . . (*No God but Allah, Mohammad is the messenger of Allah*).

لا اله الاّ اللّه محمّد رسول الله

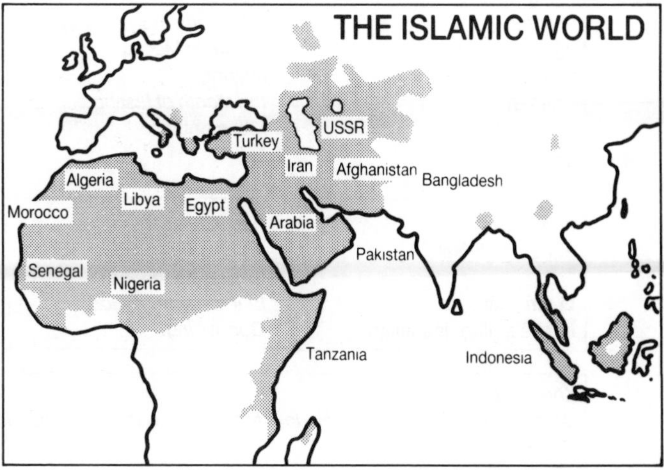

16 Religion

16.1	Islám	*Islam* (= submission)
	Alláh	*Allah, God*
	Muḥámmad	*Mohammed*
	nábī	*prophet*
	rasúl	*envoy/messenger* (from God)
	al-qur'án	*The Koran*

16.2	múslim	*Muslim*
	jámiʕ	*great mosque*
	másjid	*mosque*
	má'dhana, manára	*minaret*
	mu'ádhdhin	*muezzin* (man who calls for prayers)
	minbar	*pulpit*
	imám	*Imam* (prayer leader)
	miḥráb	*prayer corner* (towards Mecca)
	sajjáda	*prayer mat*

16.3	Mákka	*Mecca*
	al-káʕba	*the Caaba* (holy shrine)
	ḥajj	*pilgrim to Mecca*
	ṣádaqa	*charity*
	ramaḍán	*the month of fasting* (9th month)
	hiján	*veil*

ánā masíḥī.	*I am Christian.*
al-ḥámdu li-'llāh.	*Thanks be to God.* (praise be to God)
bi-smi-'lláh.	*In the name of God.*
in shá'a 'llāh, inshállāh.	*God willing.*

Koran 18.
Do not say of anything: 'I will do it tomorrow,' without adding: 'If God wills.'

Religion 16

Read these Arabic words. What do they mean?

نبي

1. ....

القرآن

2. ....

جامع

3. ....

محراب

4. ....

رمضان

5. ....

حاج

6. ....

16 Religion

- **Mohammed** (Peace be upon him)
  - c.570 Born in Mecca. Orphaned at 6. Grew up with his grandfather then with his uncle.
  - 595 Married the widow of a trader (Khadija. By her, had 2 sons who died young, and 4 daughters (one of whom was Fatima). Business trip to Syria.
  - 610 Called to be prophet by visions and voices. God's revelations to his prophet Mohammed form the Koran.
  - 622 Emigration from Mecca to Medina. In Medina became politician and statesman. Military victories followed. Defended Medina, conquered Mecca (629).
  - 632 Died in Medina after a short illness.
- The **religious duties** of Muslims (the '5 pillars' of Islam):
  1. Creed
  2. Five prayers every day. Worship on Friday in the great mosque.
  3. Alms.
  4. Daily fasts in Ramadan.
  5. Pilgrimage to Mecca.

- The **Koran**

A collection of the revelations which came to Mohammed from time to time. 114 chapters (suras) ordered by the length of their text. Sura 96 is the longest revelation. Final editing took place in 653 under the caliph Ottiman with help from Mohammed's secretary Said Thabit.
The beginning of the Koran:

الحمد للّه ربّ العالمين الرحمان الرحيم

Al-ḥámdu lillā́hi rabbi 'l-ʕā́lamīna, 'r-raḥmā́n, 'r-raḥīmi . . . (*Praise be to God, Lord of the Universe, the Compassionate, the Merciful*).

17.1 Scenery. – 17.2 At the seaside. – 17.3 Photography. – 17.4 The weather

17 The Countryside

17.1

baḥr	*sea*
al-baḥr al-áḥmar	*The Red Sea (lit.* The sea the red)
nahr	*river*
an-Nīl	*The Nile*

النيل līn-la ←

wấdī	*valley*
jabấl	*mountain/mountains*
saḥrāʾ	*desert*
sábkha	*salt lake*
nákhla	*palm tree*

17.2

shaṭṭ	*beach, coast*
shamsíyya	*sun umbrella*
másbaḥ	*swimming pool*
istiḥmấm	*bathing*
mamnúʕ al-istiḥmấm	*no bathing*
ténis	*tennis*

17.3

kámera	*camera*
film/aflấm	*film/films*

múmkin altáqit sūra?	*May I take a photograph?*

17.4

ṭaqs	*weather*
shams	*sun*
ḥārr, sukhn	*warm, hot*
bấrid	*cool*
ʕấṣifa	*storm*
máṭar	*rain*

urīd . . .	*I'd like . . .*
. . . krēmat shams	*. . . some sun cream.*
. . . naẓẓấrat shams	*. . . a pair of sunglasses.*

What can you see on these postcards?
Answer in Arabic.

1. .... أطلاس

2. .... النيل

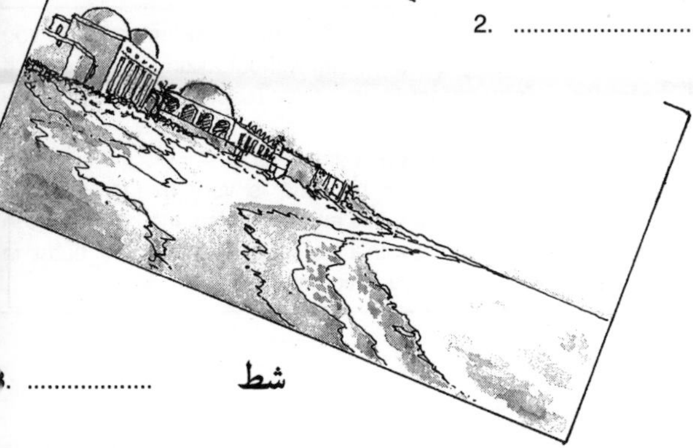

3. .... شط

17 The Countryside

It's hot. You want
to buy the following:

4. .... 5. .... 6. ....

7. You have just arrived at the hotel and ask at reception where th swimming pool is:

   ....

8. You want to photograph someone, so you ask:

   ....

What are these in Arabic?

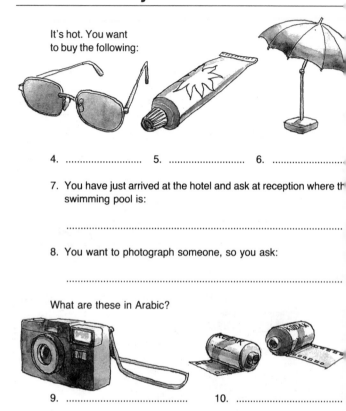

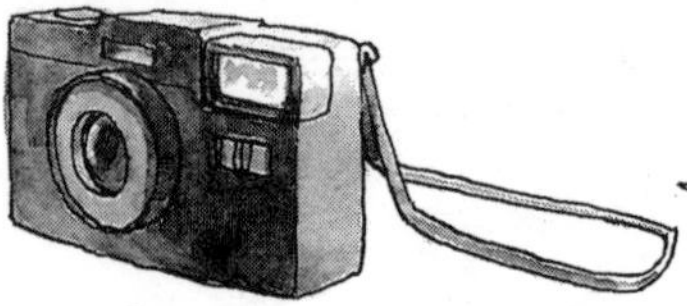

9. .... 10. ....

- The Koran forbids pictures of God, people or animals. So you should not photograph a Muslim without asking permission. If permission is not granted, you must respect it, otherwise you may get into difficulties with the police.
- In Arab countries, nudism is unthinkable.
- The widespread disease bilharzia is very dangerous. The germs are in lakes and rivers and they infect the body through the skin. Avoid contact with infected water and do not bathe in lakes or rivers under any circumstances!

18.1 Post. – 18.2 Stamps. – 18.3 Telephone.

18 Post, Telephone

18.1 al-baríd — *post*

البريد   dīr(a)b-la ←

máktab al-baríd — *post office*
ṣundúq al-baríd — *post box*

áyna máktab al-baríd?	*Where can I find a post office?*

18.2 biṭáqat baríd, kart bōstál — *postcard*
risála — *letter*

رسالة   alās(i)r ←

ṭábiaʕ/ṭawábiaʕ al-baríd — *stamp/stamps*

طوابع   ʕibāw(a)ṭ ←

al-ʕinwān — *address*
ẓarf — *envelope*

uríd ṭawábiʕ baríd	*I'd like some stamps*
. . . ílā ingíltirā	*. . . for England.*
kam?	*How much?*
ṭábiʕ wáḥid.	*A stamp*
khámas ṭawábiʕ.	*5 stamps*
uríd ṭawábiʕ kháṣa.	*I'd like some special stamps.*

18.3 hátif, tilifón — *telephone*

هاتف   f(i)tah ←

áyna 'l-hátif?	*Where can I find a telephone?*
múmkin atálfin . . . ila 'l-funduq?	*I'd like to telephone the hotel.*
raqm hátifī . . .	*My telephone number . . .*

What are these in Arabic?

1. .... 2. ....

3. .... 4. ....

5. ....

6. You are looking for the post office and ask a passer-by:

....

18 Post, Telephone

You see this sign over a post office counter:

7. What do you get here?..

8. You show the post office official your postcards and ask for stamps to England:

   ....

9. He asks you how many you want:...

10. You reply that you want 5 stamps.

    ....

11. You notice that there are pretty stamps and would like some.

    ....

12. What is this in Arabic?

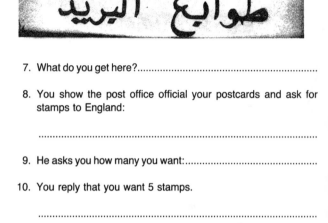

    ....

13. You are looking for a telephone and ask the receptionist:

    ....

14. Read the Arabic script. What does it mean?

    الهاتف: (07)21.797

    ....

19.1 Clothing. – 19.2 Colours. – 19.3 Hygiene. – 19.4 Jewellery

19.1	jallába	*light wrap*
	búrnus	*hooded coat*
	qafṭān	*long, embroidered dress*
	qamís	*(over) shirt*
	sirwāl	*Arab trousers*
	ḥizám	*belt*
	hátta, kaffíyya	*headscarf (for men)*
	quṭn	*cotton*
	ḥarír	*silk*
	ṣūf	*wool*
	sándal/sanấdil	*sandal/sandals*
	áḥdhiya	*shoes*
19.2	ákhḍar, khaḍrấʾ	*green* (male, female)
	áḥmar, ḥamrấʾ	*red*
	áṣfar, safrấʾ	*yellow*
	ázraq, zarqấʾ	*blue*
	ábyaḍ, baiḍấʾ	*white*
	áswad, sawdấʾ	*black*

uríd . . .	*I'd like . . .*
. . . qamís ábyaḍ	*. . . a white shirt.*
. . . qafṭấn ázraq	*. . . a blue kaftan.*

19.3	mínshafa	*towel*
	ṣābűn	*soap*
	mushṭ	*comb*
	ríḥa	*perfume*
19.4	khúmsa	*Hand of Fatima* (hand-shaped charm)
	khấtim	*ring*
	dháhab	*gold*
	fiḍḍa	*silver*
	jamíl (masc.) jamíla (fem.)	*beautiful*

al-hấtim jamíl	*The ring is beautiful.*
hấdhā dháhab?	*Is that gold?*
kam as-siʕr?	*What's the price?*

19 Clothes, Hygiene

What are these in Arabic?

1. قفطان

2. قميص

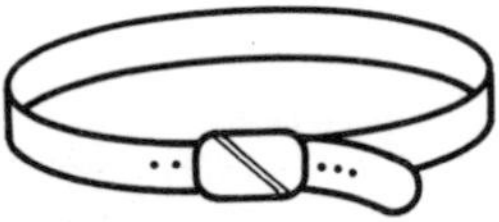

3. حزام

4. أحذية

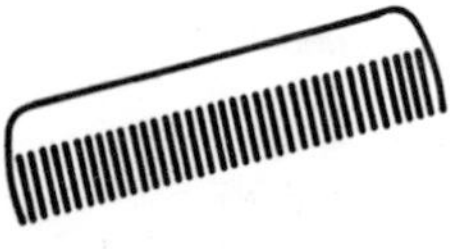

5. مشط

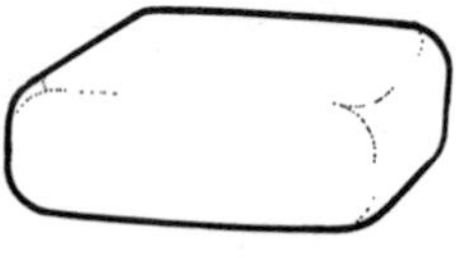

6. صابون

You are walking in Suq (the market) and see a ring which you like:

7. Say that the ring is beautiful:

....

8. Ask if it is gold:

....

9. Ask how much it costs:

....

Finally you go into a clothes shop.

10. You want to buy a white shirt:

....

11. You want to buy a blue kaftan:

....

- It is frowned upon for tourists to go around in bikinis, short-sleeved T-shirts, miniskirts and shorts when not in their hotels. Muslims regard this as being almost nudity and are not amused by it. Even the men wear long trousers outside their hotels.
- It is illegal to take pornography into an Arab country.

Koran
Enjoin believing men to turn their eyes away from temptation and to restrain their carnal desires. This will make their lives purer. Allah has knowledge of all their actions. Enjoin believing women to turn their eyes away from temptation and to preserve their chastity; to cover their adornments (except such as are normally displayed); to draw their veils over their bosoms and not to reveal their finery except to their husbands, their fathers, their husbands' fathers . . .

20 Emergencies

20.1 sáriq — *thief*
sáriqa — *robbery*

saraqū́nī	*I have been robbed . . .*
. . . miḥfáẓatī	*. . . they stole my wallet.*
. . . jawā́z sáfarī	*. . . they stole my passport.*

20.2 ash-shúrṭa/al-būlī́s — *police*

shúrṭ/būlī́s — *policeman*
muḥā́mī — *lawyer*
qā́ḍī — *judge*

múmkin atálfin . . .	*I'd like to phone . . .*
. . . ílā 'l-qunṣulíyya?	*. . . the consulate.*

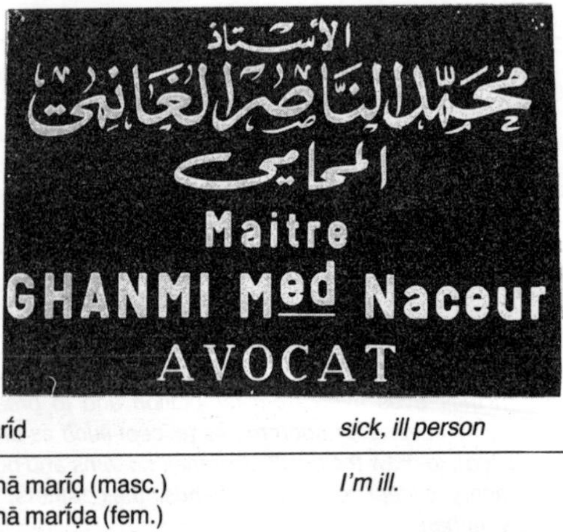

20.3 maríḍ — *sick, ill person*

ánā maríḍ (masc.)	*I'm ill.*
ánā maríḍa (fem.)	
ásh'ur biwajáaʕ húnā	*It hurts here* (point to a part of your anatomy).

20.4 ṣaydalíyya — *chemist's*

áyna áqrab ṣaydalíyya	*Where is the nearest chemist?*

20.5 ṭabíb — *doctor*

طبيب ← bib(a)ṭ

doktōr	*doctor*
ṭabíb asnán	*dentist*
mustáshfā	*hospital*

úṭlub ṭabíb, min fádlak.	*Call a doctor, please.*
tujíʕ-nī asnán-ī	*I've got toothache.*

20.6 kháṭar — *attention, danger*

Answers

1 General Expressions
1 sáyyidī 2 áhlan wa-sáhlan 3 maʕa 's-salā́ma 4 as-salāmu ʕaláykum 5 wa-ʕaláykumu s-salā́m 6 ibnī Muḥámmad 7 ibnatī Fā́ṭima 8 záwjatī Sylvia 9 náʕam, min fáḍlak 10 lā shúkran 11 ʕáfwan

2 Entering an Arab country
1 al-jawā́z min fáḍlak 2 ánta inglī́zī 3 náʕam ánā inglī́zī 4 ism-ak? 5 ism-ī Smith 6 murā́qabat al-jamā́rik 7 íftaḥ ash-shánṭa 8 lā áfham sháiʾan 9 ḥaqī́ba 10 shánṭa 11 Briṭā́nya al-ʕuẓmā

3 Travelling by car
1 sayyā́ra 2 karawā́n 3 motṓr 4 shámʕa 5 ʕájala 6 qirāʾ as-sayyārā́t 7 urī́d astáʾjir sayyāra 8 kam as-siʕr li-yawm wā́ḥid? 9 úktub hā́dhā, min fáḍlak 10 áyna maḥáṭṭat al-binzī́n? 11 Shell 12 thalāthī́n litr min fáḍlak 13 ʕábbi min fáḍlak 14 áyna garrā́j Peugeot 15 qif 16 maḥáṭṭat sayyārā́t

4 Finding your way
1 urī́d kharī́ṭa min fáḍlak 2 áyna 'ṭ-ṭarī́q ílā Tūnis? 3 urī́d kharī́ṭat al-madī́na 4 áyna ṭarī́q wásaṭ al-madī́na 5 wásaṭ al-madī́na 6 bāb ʕalī́wa 7 bāb al-madī́na 8 street map 9 street 10 street 11 left 12 right

5 Public Transport
1 ílā fúnduq Meridian, min fáḍlak 2 kif húnā, min fáḍlak 3 kam, min fáḍlak? 4 ílā al-maḥáṭṭa, min fáḍlak 5 tádhkara ílā 'l-Qā́hira 6 tadhkaratáyn ílā al-Qā́hira 7 tádhkarat metro 8 áyna máwqif at-táksī 9 ílā al-maṭā́r, min fáḍlak 10 al-irshādā́t 11 adh-dhahā́b/as-sáfar 12 jámal

6 Accommodation
1 áyna fúnduq Mīrāmār? 2 istiqbā́l 3 urī́d ghurfa li-shakhṣ wā́ḥid 4 urī́d ghurfa li-shakhṣáyn 5 kam as-siʕr li-yawm wā́ḥid? 6 sarī́r 7 miftā́ḥ 8 ḥammā́m 9 mirḥā́ḍ 10 áyna l-mirḥā́ḍ? 11 waraq al-mirḥā́ḍ? 12 al-miftā́ḥ, min fáḍlak 13 raqm thalāthīn 14 bill 15 al-ḥisā́b, min fáḍlak

7 Counting
1 2 3 4 5 one 6 twenty-five 7 ten 8 10 Dirhams 9 Morocco 10 (a) thalāth miʾat mitr (b) miʾtáy mitr (c) khams miʾat mitr (d) tisʕ miʾat mitr (e) miʾa wa sítta wa-ʕishrīn kī́lomitr 11 kīlō ṭamā́ṭim, min fáḍlak 12 kīlō burtuqā́l, min fáḍlak

8 Times and dates
1 ṣabā́ḥ 2 láyl 3 sā́ʕa 4 daqī́qa 5 kam as-sā́ʕa? 6 ath-thā́niya 7 ath-thā́niya wa-'n-niṣf 8 ath-thā́niya ʕashra 9 ath-thā́niya ʕashra 10 al-ithnáyn, ath-thulāthā́, al-arbaʕā́, al-khamī́s, al-júmʕa, as-sabt, al-áḥad 11 hádha 'l-masā́ʾ 12 ghádan ṣabā́ḥan

9 Money and Shopping
1 áyna 'l-bank 2 ṣarf 3 khams miʾat giné stirlī́nī 4 Dirham 5 Dinar 6 Dinar 7 giné 8 múmkin ashū́f as-sajjā́da al-jamī́la 9 kam as-sajjā́da? 10 úktub hā́dhā, min fáḍlak! 11 khams miʾat dīnā́r 12 ghā́lī kattī́r! 13 ánta ghanī́ wa ánā faqī́r! 14 urī́d as-sajjā́da

10 Meals
1 fuṭū́r 2 ghadā́, 3 ʕashā́ʾ 4 finjā́n 5 ṣaḥn 6 kās 7 sikkīn 8 zujā́ja 9 mílʕaqa 10 sháwka 11 qáhwa 12 ḥalī́b 13 ʕásal 14 zubda

11 Restaurants
1 máṭʕam Barrouṭa 2 yā sáyyid 3 urī́d ā́kul shaiʾ 4 mā́dhā turī́d an táshrab? 5 milḥ 6 harī́sa 7 al-ḥisā́b, min fáḍlak 8 hā́dhā lak

12 Soups, meat, fish
1 makarū́na 2 eskalṓp 3 kíbda 4 sámak máshwī 5 dajā́j bi-r-ruzz 6 omlḗt 7 shū́rba 8 sámak 9 kharū́f 10 dajā́j 1 sámak

13 Vegetables, fruit, desserts
1 burtuqā́l 2 laymū́n 3 baṭā́ṭā 4 báṣal 5 ṭamā́ṭim 6 mī́shmish 7 mawz 8 baṭṭī́kh 9 shokōlā́ta bi-'l-ḥalī́b 10 baṭṭī́kha 11 khámas burtuqālā́t 12 kī́lō ṭamā́ṭim

14 Drinking and Smoking
1 Fanta, Coca Cola 2 mā' máʕdinī 3 Kola 4 gazóza 5 ʕaṣír burtuqā́l 6 shāy bi-' laymū́n 7 qáhwa ḥílwa 8 ʕíndak bīra? 9 bī́ra stīllā, min fáḍlak 10 No smoking

15 Sightseeing
1 Kartaja 2 Tunisia 3 Egypt 4 raqṣ shárqī 5 trips 6 open 7 exit 8 cinema

16 Religion
1 Prophet 2 Koran 3 Grand Mosque 4 prayer corner 5 Ramadan 6 Pilgrim (who went to Mecca)

17 The Countryside
1 jabā́l 2 an-Nīl 3 shaṭʕ 4 naẓẓā́rat shams 5 krēmat shams 6 shamsíyya 7 áina 'il-másbaḥ 8 múmkin áltaqit sūra? 9 kámera 10 aflā́m

18 Post and Telephone
1 ṭabiʕ barī́d 2 kart bóstā́l 3 al ʕinwan 4 ẓarf 5 ṣandū́q al-barī́d 6 áyna máktab al-barī́d? 7 postage stamps 8 ṭawā́biʕ ílā ingiltira 9 kam ṭā́biʕ 10 khamas ṭawā́biʕ min fáḍlak 11 urī́d ṭawā́biʕ khā́ṣṣa 12 tilifṓn 13 áina al-tilifṓn? 14 telephone

19 Clothes and Hygiene
1 qafṭā́n 2 qamī́s 3 hizā́m 4 áḥdhiya 5 mushṭ 6 ṣābū́n 7 al-khā́tim jamī́l 8 hā́dhā dháhab? 9 kam as-siʕr? 10 urī́d qamī́s ábyaḍ 11 urī́d qafṭā́n ázraq

Arabic–English Glossary

ábyaḍ *white* 19.2
ábu 'l-hawl *sphinx* 15.2
ákhḍār *green* 19.2
ʕáfwan *excuse me* 1.3
al-áḥad *Sunday* 8.2
áḥmar *red* 19.2
áyna *where* 4.3
ʕájala *wheel* 3.1
-ak *you* 1.5
akl *food* 10.1
al- *the* 1.5
Allā́h *God* 16.1
ams *yesterday* 8.2
ánā *I* 1.5
ántā *you (m)* 1.5
ánti *you (f)* 1.5
ánta *you* 1.5
al-arbaʕāʾ *Wednesday* 8.2
ázraq *blue* 19.2
ʕashāʾ *evening meal* 10.1
ʕásal *honey* 10.3
áṣfar *yellow* 19.2
ʕāṣifa *storm* 17.4
ʕaṣī́r *juice* 14.1
ʕaṣī́r burtuqā́l *orange juice* 14.1
áswad *black* 19.2
āthār *antiquities* 15.2

bāb *city gate/gate/door* 4.2
bāb al-madī́na *city gate* 15.2
bakhshī́sh *tip* 11.3
baḥr *sea* 17.1
al-baḥr al-áḥmar *Red Sea* 17.1
báyḍa *egg* 12.3
bayt *house* 4.2
baqlā́wa *puff pastry* 13.3
bálad/bilā́d *country/countries* 2.3
bank *bank* 9.2
bā́rid *cool* 17.4
barī́d *post office* 18.1
bāṣ *bus* 5.4
báṣal *onions* 13.1
baṭā́ṭā *potatoes* 13.1
baṭṭī́kh *melons* 13.2
baṭṭāriya *battery* 3.1
binzī́n *petrol* 3.2
bīr *well* 15.2
bī́ra *beer* 14.2
bisílla *peas* 13.1
biṭā́qat barī́d *postcard* 18.2
bū́ẓa *ice cream* 13.3
búkra *tomorrow* 8.2
būlī́s *police* 20.2
búrnus *hooded coat* 19.1
burtuqā́l *oranges* 13.2

ḍābiṭ būlī́s *policeman* 20.2
dajā́ja *chicken* 12.3
daqī́qa *minute* 8.1
dalī́l as-suwwā́ḥ *guide book* 15.1
dār *house* 4.2
dīnā́r *Dinar* 9.1
dírham *Dirham (unit of currency in some Arab countries)* 9.1
diskotḗk *disco* 15.3
doktṓr *doctor* 20.5
dukhā́n *tobacco* 14.3
dukhū́l *entrance* 15.4
dukkā́n *shop* 9.3
dūsh *shower* 6.2
dhahā́b *trip* 5.2
dháhab *gold* 19.4

eskalṓp *schnitzel* 12.2

faqī́r *poor* 9.1
fármala *brake* 3.1
fātū́ra *bill* 6.3/11.3
fíḍḍa *silver* 19.4
fílfil *pepper* 11.2
film *film* 17.3
finjā́n *cup* 10.2
fúnduq *hotel* 6.1
fuṭū́r *breakfast* 10.1

gazṓza *lemonade/fizzy drink* 14.1
gatṓ *pastry/cake/gateau* 13.3
gínē *pound* 9.1
ghadāʾ *lunch* 10.1
ghádan *tomorrow* 8.2
ghā́lī *expensive* 9.4
ghanī́ *rich* 9.1
ghrām *gram* 7.2
ghúrfa *room* 6.2

harī́sa *paprika* 11.2
hā́tif *telephone* 18.3
hijā́b *veil* 16.3
húnā *here* 4.3
hunā́k *there* 4.3
ḥajj *pilgrimage to Mecca/pilgrim* 16.3
ḥaqī́ba *suitcase* 2.1
ḥalī́b *milk* 10.3/14.1
ḥammā́m *bath* 6.2
ḥáram *pyramid* 15.2
ḥarī́r *silk* 19.1
ḥarr *hot (spicy)* 11.2
hot 17.4
ḥátta *headscarf (for men)* 19.1
ḥidhaʾ *shoe/shoes* 19.1
ḥilwiyyā́t *sweets/sweet cakes* 11.1
ḥizā́m *belt* 19.1
ḥisā́b *bill* 6.3/11.3

-ī *my* 1.5
ibrī́q *jar* 10.2
al-ʕīd al-kabī́r *sacrificial feast* 15.3
-ik *you/you/to you* 1.5

Arabic–English Glossary

íla *to* 4.3
imā́m *Imam* 16.2
irshādā́t *information* 5.2
islā́m *Islam* 16.1
ism *name* 2.2
istiḥmā́m *bathing/having a bath* 17.2
istiqbā́l *reception* 6.1
al-ithnáyn *Monday* 8.2

jallā́ba *Arab dress* 19.1
jámal *camel* 5.4
jā́miʕ *mosque* 15.2/16.2
jamī́l *beautiful* 19.4
jázar *carrots* 13.1
jawā́z *passport* 2.2
jawā́z as-sáfar *passport* 2.2
jibā́l *mountain* 17.1
jilā́tī *ice cream* 13.3
jinsíyya *nationality* 2.3
jubn *cheese* 10.3
júbna *piece of cheese* 10.3
al-júmʕa *Friday* 8.2
jumhūríyya *republic* 2.3
júmruk *customs* 2.1

al-káʕba *Caaba* 16.3
kaʕk *biscuits/cake* 13.3
kabā́b *lamb kebab* 12.2
kabā́b bi'r-ruzz *kebab with rice* 12.2
kabī́na *cabin* 5.3
kabī́r *large* 15.2
kaffíyya *headscarf (for men)* 19.1
kam *how much? how many?* 7.2
kámera *camera* 17.3
kammū́n *cumin* 11.2
karawā́n *caravan* 3.1
kart bōstā́l *postcard* 18.2
kās *glass* 10.2
kíbda *liver* 12.2
kibrī́t *matches* 14.3
kīlō *kilo* 7.2
kīlumítr *kilometre* 7.2
kirāʾ as-sayyārā́t *car hire* 3.4
konyák *cognac* 14.2
kroasṓn *croissant* 10.3
-kum *your* 1.5
kuskus *couscous* 13.1
khall *vinegar* 11.2
al-khamī́s *Thursday* 8.2
khamr *wine/alcohol* 14.2
kharī́ṭah *map* 4.1
kharī́ṭat ṭúruq *street map* 4.1
kharī́ṭat al-madī́na *town plan* 4.1
kharū́f *mutton, lamb* 12.2
khā́tim *ring* 19.4
kháṭar *attention, danger* 20.6
khubz *bread* 10.3
khúḍar *vegetables* 13.1
khúmsa *Hand of Fatima (hand-shaped charm)* 19.4

khurū́j *exit* 15.4
kuzbara *coriander* 11.2

lā *no* 1.1
lában *sour milk* 10.3
laḥm/lahma *meat* 12.2
laḥm báqar *beef* 12.2
lahm kharū́f *mutton/lamb* 12.2
láila *night* 8.2
laimū́n *lemons/limes* 13.2
lawz *almond* 13.2
litr *litre* 7.2
lū́biyā *beans* 13.1

māʾ *water* 14.1
maʾ li-'sh-shurb *drinking water* 14.1
maʾ máʕdinī *mineral water* 14.1
máʕbad *temple* 15.2
máʕa 's-salā́ma *goodbye* 1.2
madī́na *town/city* 4.1
mádrasa *school* 15.2
maʾdhana *minaret* 16.2
maftū́ḥ *open* 15.4
maḥáṭṭa *station* 5.1
maḥáṭṭat binzī́n *petrol station* 3.2
maḥáṭṭat sayyārā́t *car park* 3.3
makarū́na *noodles* 12.1
Mákka *Mecca* 16.3
máktab al-barī́d *post office* 18.1
maqhā *café* 11.1
mámlaka *kingdom* 2.3
mamnū́ʕ al-istihmā́m *No bathing* 17.2
mamnū́ʕ al-wuqū́f *No parking* 3.3
manā́ra *minaret* 16.2
márḥabā *welcome/hello* 1.2
marī́d *ill/ill person* 20.3
mashrū́b *drink* 14.1
masā́ʾ *evening* 8.2
masā́ʾan *in the evening* 8.2
másbah *swimming pool* 17.2
másjid *mosque* 16.2
mátā *when* 8.2
máṭʕam *restaurant* 11.1
máṭar *rain* 17.4
maṭā́r *airport* 5.2
mát-ḥaf *museum* 15.2
al-mát-ḥaf al-mísrī *Egyptian museum* 15.2
máwqif *bus stop/car park* 5.4
máwqif tāksiyyā́t *taxi rank* 5.4
mawz *bananas* 13.2
miftā́ḥ/mafatih *key/keys* 6.2
miḥrā́b *prayer corner* 16.2
mílʕaqa *spoon* 10.2
milḥ *salt* 11.2
min fáḍlak *please (to a man)* 1.3
min fáḍlik *please (to a woman)* 1.3
mínbar *pulpit* 16.2
mínshafa *towel* 19.3

Arabic–English Glossary

mirḥā́ḍ *toilet* 6.4
míshmish *apricots* 13.2
mísˁad *lift* 6.2
motṓr *motor* 3.1
muʾádhdhin *Muezzin (man who calls prayers)* 16.2
muḍī́fa *stewardess* 5.2
muḥā́mī *lawyer* 20.2
Muḥámmad *Mohammed* 16.1
murábbā *marmalade/jam* 10.3
murā́qabat al-júmruk *customs* 2.1
muraṭṭibā́t *bakery/refreshments* 11.1
mushṭ *comb* 19.3
múslim *Muslim* 16.2
mustáshfā *hospital* 20.5

náˁam *yes* 1.1
nábī *prophet* 16.1
nabī́dh *wine* 14.2
nā́dī láylī *nightclub* 15.3
nahj *street* 4.2
nákhla *palm tree* 17.1
nahr *river* 17.1
nargī́la *hookah/hubble bubble* 14.3
-nī *me/to me* 1.5
niṣf kīlō *half kilo* 7.2
nuqū́d *money* 9.1

omlḗt *omelette* 12.3
ōtēl *hotel* 6.1

qā́dī *judge* 20.2
qafṭā́n *long loose garment/kaftan* 19.1
qáhwa *coffee* 10.3/14.1
qamī́ṣ shirt 19.1
qárya *village* 4.2
qarnī́t *octopus, squid, cuttlefish* 12.4
qaṣba *fortified (old) town* 15.2
qaṣr *palace* 15.2
qif *stop* 3.3
qunṣulíyya *consulate* 2.3
al-Qurʾā́n *Koran* 16.1
quṭn *cotton/cotton wool* 19.1

rādiyátōr *radiator* 3.1
rā́kib *passenger* 5.2
raqs shárqī *belly dance* 15.3
ramaḍā́n *Ramadan* 16.3
rasū́l *messenger (from God)* 16.1
riḥlā́t *outings* 15.1
rī́ḥa *perfume* 19.3
risā́la *letter/message* 18.2
ruzz *rice* 13.1

sā́ˁa *hour* 8.1
sábkha *salt lake* 17.1
as-sabt *Saturday* 8.2
sáfar *journey/travel* 15.1
safī́na *ship* 5.3
sā́ḥa *square* 4.2
sayyā́ra *car* 3.1
sáyyid *gentleman (Mr)* 1.4
sáyyida *lady (Mrs)* 1.4
sáyyidī *sir* 1.4
sajjā́da *prayer mat/rug* 16.2
sak *bag* 2.1
sálaṭa *salad* 13.1
sámak/sámaka *fish/a fish* 12.4
sardī́n/sardina *sardine/a sardine* 12.4
sā́riq *thief* 20.1
sā́riqa *robbery* 20.1
sarī́r *bed* 6.2
siˁr *price* 6.3/9.4
sifā́ra *Embassy* 2.3
sigā́ra *cigarette* 14.3
síkkat al-hadī́d *railway* 5.1
sikkī́n *knife* 10.2
sínamā *cinema* 15.3
sirwā́l *Arab trousers/trunks* 19.1
stēk *steak* 12.2
sū́biyā *cuttlefish* 12.4
sukhn *hot/warm* 17.4
súkkar *sugar* 11.2
sūq *market* 9.3
sūpermarkit *supermarket* 9.3
shay *tea* 10.3/14.1
shámˁa *spark plug/candle* 3.1
shams *sun* 17.4
shamsíyya *sunshine umbrella* 17.2
shā́riˁ *avenue/street* 4.2
shaṭṭ *coast* 17.2
beach 17.2
sháwka *fork* 10.2
shik *cheque* 9.2
shī́sha *hookah* 14.3
shokōlā́ta *chocolate* 13.3
shúkran *thank you* 1.3
shúkran jazī́lan *thank you very much* 1.3
shū́rba *soup* 12.1
shúrṭa *police* 20.2
ṣabā́ḥ *morning* 8.2
ṣabā́ḥ al-khair *good morning* 1.2
ṣabā́ḥan *in the morning* 8.2
ṣābū́n *soap* 19.3
ṣádaqa *alms/voluntary gifts* 16.3
ṣaḥn *plate* 10.2
ṣaḥrā́ʾ *desert* 17.1
ṣaydalíyya *chemist* 20.4
ṣándal *sandal* 19.1
ṣarf *Bureau de change* 9.2
ṣūf *wool* 19.1
ṣundū́q al-barī́d *post box* 18.1

tábagh *tobacco* 14.3
tadkhī́n *smoking* 14.3
tádhkara *ticket* 5.1
tádhkarat al-tayyā́ra *airline ticket* 5.2
ṭayyā́ra *aeroplane* 5.2

Arabic–English Glossary

táksi *taxi* 5.4
tamr *dates* 13.2
taʾshíra *visa* 2.2
ténis *tennis* 17.2
tilifón *telephone* 18.3
tuffáḥ *apples* 13.2
tūn *tuna fish* 12.4
tháman *price* 6.3/9.4
ath-thulātháʾ *Tuesday* 8.2
thūm *garlic* 11.2
ṭábiʿ baríd *postage stamp* 18.2
ṭabíb *doctor* 20.5
ṭabíb asnán *dentist* 20.5
ṭábiq *storey* 6.2
ṭaqs *weather* 17.4
ṭamáṭim *tomatoes* 13.1
ṭaríq *way* 4.2
ṭūl,ʿala ṭūl *straight on* 4.3

ʿunwán *address* 18.2

vísā *visa* 2.2

wa- *and* 1.5
wādī *valley* 17.1
waraq al-mirḥáḍ *toilet paper* 6.4
wuṣúl *arrival* 5.2

yálla *come on* 4.3
yamín *right* 4.3
yasár *left* 4.3
yawm *day* 8.2
al-yawm *today* 8.2

zabíb *raisins* 13.2
zayt *oil* 11.2
zayt motór *motor oil* 3.2
zaytún *olives* 12.1
zúbda *butter* 10.3
zujája *bottle* 10.2

English–Arabic Glossary

address ʕunwán 18.2
aeroplane ṭayyára 5.2
airline ticket tádhkarat al-ṭayyára 5.2
airport maṭár 5.2
almonds lawz 13.2
alms ṣádaqa 16.3
and wa- 1.5
antiquities āthār 15.2
apple tuffáḥ 13.2
apricots míshmish 13.2
Arabic trousers/trunks sirwál 19.1
arrival wuṣúl 5.2
attention, danger kháṭar 20.6
avenue sháriʕ 4.2

bag sak 2.1
bananas mawz 13.2
bank bank 9.2
bath ḥammám 6.2
bathing istiḥmám 17.2
battery baṭṭāriya 3.1
beach shaṭṭ 17.2
beans lúbiyā 13.1
beautiful jamíl 19.4
bed sarír 6.2
beef laḥm baqar 12.1
beer bíra 14.2
belly dance raqṣ shárqī 15.3
belt hizám 19.1
big kabír 15.2
bill fātúra 6.3/11.3
ḥisáb 6.3/11.3
black áswad 19.2
blue ázraq 19.2
bottle zujája 10.2
brake fármala 3.1
bread khubz 10.3
breakfast fuṭúr 10.1
bureau de change ṣarf 9.2
bus bāṣ 5.4
bus stop máuqif 5.4
butter zúbda 10.3

Caaba al-káʕba 16.3
cabin kabína 5.3
café máqhā 11.1
camel jámal 5.4
camera kámera 17.3
can/jar ibríq 10.2
car hire kirā' as-sayyārát 3.4
car park maháṭṭat sayyārát 3.3
car sayyára 3.1
caravan karawán 3.1
caraway kammún 11.2
carrots jázar 13.1
cheese jubn 10.3
cheese júbna 10.3
chemist ṣaydalíyya 20.4
cheque shik 9.2

chicken dajája 12.3
chocolate shokōláta 13.3
cigarette sigára 14.3
cinema sínamā 15.3
city gate bāb 4.2
bab al-madína 15.2
coast shaṭṭ 17.2
coffee qáhwa 10.3/14.1
cognac konyák 14.2
comb mushṭ 19.3
consulate qunṣulíyya 2.3
cool bárid 17.4
coriander kazbara 11.2
cotton (wool) quṭn 19.1
country/countries balad/bilád 2.3
couscous kuskus 13.1
croissant kroasón 10.3
cumin kammún 11.2
cup finján 10.2
customs júmruk 2.1
customs control muráqabat al-júmruk 2.1
cuttlefish, squid, octopus qarnít 12.4
sūbiyā 12.4

dates tamr 13.2
day yawm 8.2
dentist ṭabíb asnán 20.5
desert ṣaḥrá' 17.1
Dinar dīnár 9.1
disco diskoték 15.3
doctor doktōr 20.5
doctor ṭabíb 20.5
door bāb 4.2
drink mashrúb 14.1
drinking water mā' li-sh-shurb 14.1

egg báiḍa 12.3
Egyptian museum al-mát-ḥaf al-míṣrí 15.2
embassy sifāra 2.3
entrance dukhúl 15.4
evening masáʕ 8.2
evening meal ʕasháʕ 10.1
excuse me ʕáfwan 1.3
exit khurúj 15.4
expensive ghálī 9.4

fasting month ramaḍán 16.3
film film 17.3
fish/a fish sámak/sámaka 12.4
food akl 10.1
fork sháwka 10.2
fortified old city qáṣba 15.2
Friday al-júmʕa 8.2

garlic thūm 11.2
gentleman sáyyid 1.4
glass kas 10.2
God Alláh 16.1
gold dháhab 19.4

English–Arabic Glossary

good morning ṣabā́ḥ al-khayr 1.2
goodbye maʕa 's-salāma 1.2
gram ghrām 7.2
great mosque jā́miʕ 15.2/16.2
green ákhḍar 19.2
guidebook dalī́l as-suwwā́ḥ 15.1

half kilo niṣf kīlō 7.2
hand of Fatima khúmsa 19.4
headscarf (for men) kaffíyya 19.1
hátta 19.1
here húnā 4.3
honey ʕásal 10.3
hooded coat búrnus 19.1
hospital mustáshfā 20.5
hot harr 11.2
hot (weather) harr 17.4
hot sukhn 17.4
hotel fúnduq 6.1
ōtēl 6.1
houkah nargī́la 14.3
shī́sha 14.3
hour sā́ʕa 8.1
house dār/bayt 4.2
how many?/how much? kam? 7.2

I ánā 1.5
ice cream bū́ẓa 13.3
jilā́tī 13.3
ill/ill person marī́ḍ 20.3
Imam imā́m 16.2
in the evening masā́ʾan 8.2
in the mornings ṣabā́ḥan 8.2
information irshādā́t 5.2
Islam islā́m 16.1

journey sáfar 15.1
judge qā́ḍī 20.2
juice ʕaṣī́r 14.1

kebab with rice kabā́b bi'r-ruzz 12.2
key miftā́ḥ 6.2
kilo kīlō 7.2
kilometre kīlumítr 7.2
kingdom mámlaka 2.3
knife sikkī́n 10.2
Koran al-qurʾā́n 16.1

lady sáyyida 1.4
lamb Kharū́f 12.2
lamb kebab kabā́b 12.2
lawyer muḥā́mī 20.2
left yasā́r 4.3
lemonade gazṓza 14.1
lemons/limes laymū́n 13.2
let's go yálla 4.3
letter risā́la 18.2
lift mísʕad 6.2
light shawl jallā́ba 19.1
litre litr 7.2
liver kíbda 12.2
long dress qafṭā́n 19.1
lunch ghadā́ʾ 10.1

map kharī́ṭa 4.1
map tádhkara 5.1
market sūq 9.3
marmalade murábbā 10.3
matches kibrī́t 14.3
me -nī 1.5
meat laḥm 12.2
meat láḥma 12.2
Mecca Mákka 16.3
melons baṭṭíkh 13.2
messenger (from God) rasū́l 16.1
milk ḥalī́b 10.3/14.1
minaret manā́ra 16.2
maʾdhana 16.2
mineral water māʾ máʕdinī 14.1
minute daqī́qa 8.1
Mohammed Muḥámmad 16.1
Monday al-ithnáyn 8.2
money nuqū́d 9.1
morning ṣabā́ḥ 8.2
mosque másjid 16.2
motor motṓr 3.1
motor oil zayt motṓr 3.2
mountain/mountains jabal/jibā́l 17.1
muezzin muʾádhdhin 16.2
museum mát-ḥaf 15.2
Muslim múslim 16.2
mutton kharū́f 12.2
mutton lahm kharū́f 12.2
my -ī 1.5

name ism 2.2
nationality jinsíyya 2.3
night láila 8.2
nightclub nā́dī láilī 15.3
no bathing mamnū́ʕ al-istihmā́m 17.2
no lā 1.1
no parking mamnū́ʕ al-wuqū́f 3.3
noodles makarū́na 12.1

oil zayt 11.2
olives zaytun 12.1
omelette omlḗt 12.3
onions báṣal 13.1
open maftū́ḥ 15.4
orange juice ʕaṣir al-burtuqal 14.1
oranges burtuqā́l 13.2

palace qaṣr 15.2
palm nákhla 17.1
paprika harī́sa 11.2
passenger rā́kib 5.2
passport jawā́z 2.2
passport jawā́z as-sáfar 2.2

pastry, cake kaaʕk 13.3
gató 13.3
peas bisílla 13.1
pepper fílfil 11.2
perfume ríḥa 19.3
petrol binzín 3.2
petrol station maḥáṭṭat binzín 3.2
pilgrimage to Mecca hajj 16.3
plate ṣaḥn 10.2
please min fáḍlak (*m*) 1.3
min fáḍlik (*f*) 1.3
police shúrṭa 20.2
policeman būlís 20.2
poor faqír 9.1
post baríd 18.1
post box sundúq al-baríd 18.1
post office máktab al-baríd 18.1
postcard kart bōstál 18.2
biṭáqat baríd 18.2
potatoes baṭáṭā 13.1
pound gínē 9.1
prayer corner mihráb 16.2
prayer mat sajjáda 16.2
price tháman 6.3/9.4
siʕr 6.3/9.4
prophet nábī 16.1
puff pastry baqláwa 13.3
pulpit mínbar 16.2
pyramid/pyramids háram/ahram 15.2

radiator rādiyátōr 3.1
railway síkkat al-ḥadíd 5.1
rain máṭar 17.4
raisins zabíb 13.2
reception istiqbál 6.1
Red Sea al-baḥr al-áḥmar 17.1
red áḥmar 19.2
refreshments muraṭṭibát 11.1
republic jumhūríyya 2.3
restaurant máṭʕam 11.1
rice ruzz 13.1
rich ghaní 9.1
right yamín 4.3
ring khátim 19.4
river nahr 17.1
robbery sáriqa 20.1
room ghúrfa 6.2

sacrificial feast al-ʕīd al-kabír 15.3
salad sálaṭa 13.1
salt lake sábkha 17.1
salt milḥ 11.2
sandals ṣándal 19.1
sardine sardína 12.4
Saturday as-sabt 8.2
schnitzel eskalóp 12.2
school mádrasa 15.2
sea baḥr 17.1
ship safína 5.3
shirt qamíṣ 19.1
shoes aḥdhiyya 19.1
shop dukkán 9.3
shower dūsh 6.2
silk ḥarír 19.1
silver fíḍḍa 19.4
sir sáyyidī 1.4
smoking tadkhín 14.3
soap ṣābún 19.3
soup shúrba 12.1
sour milk lában 10.3
spark plug/candle shámʕa 3.1
Sphinx ábu' l-hawl 15.2
spoon mílʕaqa 10.2
square ṣáḥa 4.2
stamp ṭábiʕ al-baríd 18.2
station maḥáṭṭa 5.1
steak stēk 12.2
stewardess muḍífa 5.2
stop qif 3.3
storey ṭābiq 6.2
storm ʕáṣifa 17.4
straight on ʕala ṭūl 4.3
street map kharíṭat ṭúruq 4.1
street nahj 4.2
sugar súkkar 11.2
suitcase ḥaqíba 2.1
sun shams 17.4
Sunday al-áḥad 17.4
sun umbrella shamsíyya 17.2
supermarket sūpermarkit 9.3
sweets/desserts hilwiyyát 11.1
swimming pool másbaḥ 17.2

take-off qiyám 5.2
taxi rank máwqif tāksıyyát 5.4
taxi táksī 5.4
tea shay 10.2/14.1
telephone hátif 18.3
tilifón 18.3
temple máʕbad 15.2
tennis ténis 17.2
thank you shúkran 1.3
thank you very much shúkran jazílan 1.3
the al- (*m*)
al- (*f*)
there hunák 4.3
thief sáriq 20.1
Thursday al-khamís 8.2
tip bakhshísh 1.3
to me -nī 1.5
to you -ak 1.5/-ik 1.5
to you -kum 1.5
-ik 1.5
to ílā 4.3
tobacco dukhán 14.3
ṭábagh 14.3
today al-yawm 8.2
toilet mirḥáḍ 6.4

English–Arabic Glossary

toilet paper waraq al-mirḥáḍ 6.4
tomatoes ṭamáṭim 13.1
tomorrow búkra 8.2
ghádan 8.2
towel mínshafa 19.3
town madína 4.1
town plan kharíṭat al-madína 4.1
trips riḥlāt 15.1
Tuesday ath-thulāthá' 8.2
tuna fish tūn 12.4

valley wādī 17.1
vegetable khúḍar 13.1
veil ḥijáb 16.3
village qárya 4.2
vinegar khall 11.2
visa ta'shíra 2.2
vísā 2.2

warm (weather) ḥarr 17.4
warm sukhn 17.4
water mā' 14.1
way ṭaríq 4.2
weather ṭaqs 17.4
Wednesday al-arbaʕā' 8.2
welcome márḥabā 1.2
well, fountain bīr 15.2
wheel ʕájala 3.1
when mátā 8.2
where áyna 4.3
white ábyaḍ 19.2
wine khamr 14.2
nabídh 14.2
wool ṣūf 19.1

yellow áṣfar 19.2
yes náʕam 1.1
yesterday ams 8.2
you (accusative) -ak 1.5
-ik 1.5
you ánta (*m*) 1.5
ánti (*f*) 1.5
your -ak (*m*) 1.5
-ik (*f*) 1.5
your -kum (*pl*) 1.5